PRAISE F(

F*CK YOUR COMFORT ZONE

"No one wants to be around or watch someone who is 'perfect.' And none of us are. So, f— it! Margie pushes you to bring your authentic, messy, odd, beautiful self to everything you do. Even though this book's title is swearing at you, take these words to heart." —JOHNNO WILSON, actor and comedian (*Raven's Home, Curb Your Enthusiasm*)

"You know how when you're uncomfortable you immediately insult yourself or your intelligence to break the tension? It sucks, right? I know! Margie taught me how to cut that shit out, step into myself, and stop giving away my power. And she can teach you too! God, this quote probably sucked . . . psych, it's perfect!" —DAN NUFER, actor (*Let's Make a Movie*)

"I've had a number of coaches during my time in La La Land. Margie was the first one to teach me how to wield my creative life like a superpower." —TERRELL BATTLE, actor (*Black-ish, The Good Doctor, Killing It*)

"Early on I had a lot of fears that stopped me. I remember auditioning for a musical, *The Best Little Whorehouse in Texas*. I handed the sheet music to the pianist, walked out onstage, and when I opened my mouth to sing, no sound came out. Again, the pianist played the intro, and again, no sound came out. I left the stage knowing that I had to learn how to manage myself in spite of my fears. I wish *F*ck Your Comfort Zone* had been written back then. I could have saved myself a lot of anguish and time in therapy." —TIM BAGLEY, actor (*Will & Grace, Grace and Frankie*)

"An extraordinary piece of work—relevant, timely, and hopeful!" —ZAIN VERJEE, founder and CEO, Zain Verjee Group, and former CNN anchor

"I felt so stuck trying to be 'right' and 'perfect' all the time that I forgot how to be creative. This book is a game-changer! *F*ck Your Comfort Zone* immediately!" —GINA BRAMHILL, actress (*Sherlock, Us, Endeavour*)

"I had a hate-hate relationship with auditions. Margie helped me learn how to love the process, f*ck my comfort zone, and swim in the wonderful messiness of life." —MARQUE RICHARDSON,
actor (*Dear White People, Antebellum*)

"Margie taught me to say 'fuck it' and 'love yourself.' Wake up, everyone! You, too, can find joy. Read this transformative book."
—KANDISS EDMUNDSON,
actress (*Bosch*)

"I've spent most of my life taking risks: traveling the world for authentic street food, opening and sometimes closing restaurants, writing cookbooks, and pioneering one of Food Network's first cooking shows, and I've loved all of it! Margie's book is a great reminder to reach for your dreams and enjoy the journey!" —SUSAN FENIGER,
celebrity chef, restaurateur,
cookbook author, and activist

"I spent much of my life fearful that I wouldn't be liked if I showed the 'real' me. It's so freeing to accept that I'm fine as I am, especially as a TV journalist and interviewer. Reading Margie's insightful book reinforced how imperative it is to free yourself and be in the moment."
—SUSAN NEISLOSS,
president, Big Bite Films

"My mind was swirling constantly: Look this way. Cry this way. Anger this way. Love this way. Act this way. Then I met Margie. Now, it's: Create the life. Live the life. Give that Critical Parent a hug, then tell 'em to shut the f*ck up. It's time to play! Wait till you read this book." —JACK PERRY,
musician and actor (*30 Rock, Ugly Betty*)

"Where the f*ck do I begin? Margie is a bolt of lightning who shows her actors how to take risks and have power, especially in their daily lives . . . with all my heart and honesty, read the f*cking book! I love Margie Haber . . . end scene." —FERN CHAMPION,
casting director (*The Police Academy, Naked Gun,*
Emmy-nominated miniseries *Hatfields & McCoys*)

"I tried to cover up imperfections and scars, and hid in the corner. Margie gave me the courage to live in the unknown which makes the human experience so beautiful." —EUGENIA KUZMINA,
actress (*Spy City*, Comedy Parlor Live)

"Margie helped me understand what I was capable of on the battlefield as a combat veteran and in the boardroom. A must-read for anyone seeking to understand their potential." —JUSTIN WOLFF, cofounder and CEO, Junk Theory

"Read this book! You, too, can find freedom in letting go!" —BRANDON SCOTT, actor (*Dead to Me, Goliath*)

"This book is exactly what I needed. It reminded me to be brave and take a risk to be vulnerable." —ROCHELLE AYTES, actress (*Mistresses, SWAT*)

"Margie's book helped me to let go of my armor and tap into more of my humor and vulnerability." —MELANIE NICHOLLS-KING, actress (*The Wire, Your Honor, Little Fires Everywhere*)

"If I had stayed in my comfort zone, I would not have successful careers in music and art. Margie gives you permission to achieve great things. Start with yelling out, 'F*ck my comfort zone!!'" —BILLY MORRISON, artist and guitarist for Billy Idol

"Back in the day, while casting the *Lord of the Rings* trilogy, I learned a valuable lesson. I cannot control the outcome. I can only do my job to the best of my ability and let go of the rest. Margie's book teaches you just that, and she does it in a supportive and loving way. Inspiring!" —VICTORIA BURROWS, CSA, casting director (*Lord of the Rings* trilogy, *Flight, Project Blue Book*)

"Margie's wonderful book helps everyone learn to be empathetic and curious. That is what makes a good storyteller, a good teacher, and . . . a good human being." —ELISSA DOWN, director (*Ivy and Bean, Feel the Beat, The Black Balloon*)

"Self-compassion, staying present and curious, and being empathetic can fuel your life with endless happiness and joy. Change your life. Follow Margie out of your comfort zone!" —ELYSE RESCH, nutrition therapist and coauthor (*Intuitive Eating*)

"Margie Haber's wisdom and insight into the human condition are truly profound. Do you want to learn to embrace discomfort and have fun doing it? Margie's book will guide you through it."　—RICHARD GUNN, actor (*Dark Angel, Hemlock Grove, Granite Flats*)

"As an actress on the autism spectrum, acting was a means of hiding my differences from the world. Margie's coaching gave me the courage to embrace all the parts of myself. And then I booked the series! Run, don't walk, to your bookstore. It is a life changer!"　—SUE ANN PIEN, actress (*As We See It*)

"As an NBA coach, I use Margie's lesson: 'When you push past your comfort, then you find greatness.'"　—LINDSEY HARDING, head coach, South Sudan basketball program, and former assistant coach, Sacramento Kings

"Powerful . . . and impacted me in subtle and profound ways."　—DR. MINDY E. GOLDMAN, gynecologist and director, Gynecology Center for Cancer Survivors and At-Risk Women, UCSF Health

"An inspiring call to action, helping us all to tell our inner fear and critic to 'shut the f*ck up.'"　—DAKOTA GORMAN, writer, director, and actress (*All About Sex*)

"Profound life advice."　—MICHAEL CORBETT, producer, writer, and Emmy-winning actor

"After reading the book, I bought a ticket to LA! It was the best decision of my life."　—ALICE TORRIANI, actress, author, and screenwriter

"Every hiccup, mistake, or imperfection is a gift in disguise. Margie will help you pick yourself up and try again while reminding you to laugh along the way."　—KEELIA FLINN, actress and producer (*My Crazy Sex*)

"Margie taught me how to use the 'F' words—Fall Forward into Fear."　—TAYLOR CARTER, actress (*Snare*)

MARGIE HABER

HOLLYWOOD'S TOP ACTING COACH

F*ck YOUR Comfort ZONE

TAKE A RISK AND BECOME THE LEAD IN YOUR OWN LIFE

Regan Arts.

NEW YORK

Regan Arts.

Copyright © Margie Haber, 2022

All rights reserved, including the right to reproduce this book or portions thereof in any form whatsoever. For information, contact internationalrights@reganarts.com.

This book is a memoir. It reflects the author's recollections of experiences over time. Some names and characteristics may have been changed, some events have been compressed, and some dialogue has been recreated. Regan Arts is committed to publishing works of quality and integrity. We are proud to publish this book; however, the story, the experiences, and the words are the author's alone.

Although the author and publisher have made every effort to ensure that the information in this book is correct, the author and publisher do not assume and hereby disclaim any liability to any party for any loss, damage, or disruption caused by errors or omissions, whether such errors or omissions result from negligence, accident, or any other cause. This book is not intended as a substitute for psychological or medical advice from physicians. The reader should regularly consult a physician in matters relating to his/her health. The author has tried to recreate events and conversations from her memories of them. In order to maintain anonymity in some instances, she has changed the names of individuals. She may have changed some identifying characteristics and details such as physical properties, occupations, and places of residence.

First Regan Arts paperback edition, May 2022

Library of Congress Control Number: 2021944730

ISBN 978-1-68245-196-0 (Paperback)
ISBN 978-1-68245-217-2 (Paperback Second Edition 2023)
ISBN 978-1-68245-197-7 (eBook)

Interior design by Aubrey Khan, Neuwirth & Associates, Inc.
Cover Design by Richard Ljoenes

Author photo credit © Steven Busby

Mary Wilson and Margie Haber photo credit © Tracey Landworth

Excerpt p. 134–135 from *Late, Late at Night* by Rick Springfield. Copyright © 2010 by Rick Springfield. Reprinted with permission from Touchstone, a division of Simon & Schuster, Inc.

Printed in the United States of America

For my Supreme, my best friend, Mary Wilson,
who spent her life living outside of her comfort zone.

You touched so many people and lovingly introduced me
to a life I may have never had without knowing you.

You are greatly missed.

CONTENTS

x Contents

*

INTRODUCTION

I wrote this book during an unprecedented time, the coronavirus pandemic. Our lives have been thrown into chaos. We wear masks, stand six feet apart, and many of us have not experienced the touch of loved ones, nor have we been able to shake hands with strangers. We applaud the people on the front lines—health care workers, journalists, police, firefighters, and all essential workers, who take risks every day to keep us safe. They are our heroes. Now, it's time for you to become the hero of your own life by removing your facade, embracing your imperfections, and igniting your courage.

In my long career as an acting coach and teacher, I've met and worked with thousands of people from diverse walks of life. And I've found we have one thing in common. It's a straightjacket we each wear called our "comfort zone." It's where we think we are safe, but it turns out to be a personal prison of our own making. There is nothing that robs a person of happiness and a feeling of power more than existing, day in and day out, in a comfort zone. The comfort zone is predictable, boring, and stagnant. We all can feel that a more invigorating and creative life exists outside of the zone, but the gate guard of fear stops us in our tracks.

Here's my number one coaching tip:

F*ck Your Comfort Zone.
What has it done for you lately?

You've stood on the sidelines, played the extra, served as a stand-in, and disappeared on the third balcony, row LL, seat 119, for far too long. Fuck it! Take risks. It's time to become the lead in your *own* life. When you've coasted in neutral in any area of your life, professional or personal, a playful "fuck it!" can become your freedom cheer. It always produces a genuine reaction that breaks through our self-imposed restrictions.

We all struggle with the same challenges—whether we're a Fortune 500 executive, a teacher, contractor, chef, parent, social worker, actor, or any person—to be seen, to be heard, to have meaningful relationships, and to be vulnerable and open.

Every person shares the happiness-destroying gate guard called fear. Fear bites. Fear trips us up. Fear keeps us living small. Fear is an embarrassing thing to admit to as an adult, so we avoid it and languish in our comfort zone straightjackets.

First, this book will help you identify your personal comfort zone. Then, it will give you practical applications to harness your fear and use it for good to increase your power in all capacities: healthier relationships, giving voice to your truth, enjoying your talents and skills, living in the present, and, most importantly, being happy. And, no matter what your ambition or goal in life might be, isn't happiness the brass ring we all want to grab?

I've worked with some big names in Hollywood: Halle Berry, Brad Pitt, Vince Vaughn, Kyle Chandler, Mariska Hargitay, Tiffany Haddish, and countless others. These are people who may exude star quality on the screen and in public, but also share the exact same trepidation and fear as you and me. Success, for each of them, eventually happened because they were curious about their discomfort and willing to live in it, to use their fear to propel them into the unknown. They found immense power and satisfaction while being vulnerable.

In the 1990s, Heather Locklear sat in the corner of my classroom, buried in an oversized sweatshirt, praying I wouldn't call on her. But when I did, she found her voice and stepped out of hiding, bravely falling forward.

Six days a week, I coach actors, business professionals, writers, day workers, stay-at-home parents, and anyone looking for a way to live more fully and authentically.

The essence of my teaching, and this book, is:

When you start turning your fear into risk-taking energy and stretch out of your comfort zone, you can begin to approach life with empathy and curiosity toward yourself and others. It changes everything.

I've witnessed effective and joyful transformations with countless people, and I believe that with each chapter of this book, you're going to find hope for yourself. Have no fear. It won't be jarring or overwhelming. Becoming the lead in your life is not a one-time achievement; it's a steady progression of small victories)

I'm the "small victories" poster child. I've been in therapy for more than half of my life. On these pages, I'm even sharing a few of my personal therapy sessions, revealing my own fears and struggles. You'll also read some in-class experiences with my students and their personal stories, challenges, and breakthroughs. As you'll soon see, you're not alone.

F*ck Your Comfort Zone will provide you with a plan to overcome personal obstacles, along with my "Margisms," which are simple self-guides that you can apply to your life tomorrow and every day—one small victory at a time.

At the end of each chapter are writing exercises specifically designed to help you shatter unhealthy thought patterns, obliterate cycles of behavior that no longer serve you, and replace bad habits with good ones. The odyssey you are about to embark on will be fueled by kindness, especially to yourself.

I encourage you to embrace what is rightfully yours by taking off your comfort zone straightjacket. Open your life to more happiness.

You got this!

1

To Be or Not to Be . . . in Control

My life was certainly unpredictable when I accepted a teaching job in Jakarta, Indonesia. Everyone was warning me of the danger, especially as a Jewish American woman who is gay. They freaked me out so much that I even bought a purse with a Canadian symbol on it.

On the first day in Jakarta, forty adults, the majority of them Muslim, entered my classroom. I had taken the risk to be there, so I knew I had to also risk being my true self, Margie Haber.

The first thing I did was tell them who I am. I "outed" myself completely, in all aspects, and they embraced me. There was no scary or dangerous aftermath, only acceptance. I became familiar with Muslim practices and, in turn, embraced them. During our lunch breaks, they would leave for an hour to pray. Being Jewish, I ate pizza.

My first exercise for the class involved taking them back to their childhood to find an object in their bedroom. While their eyes were closed, I heard a terrible sobbing and realized it was coming from a student named Jodie. I asked everyone to open his or her eyes and be present with us while I knelt down to comfort her.

Jodie shared her childhood experience with the class: "When I was six, I was confined in a medical bubble in the hospital due to a very rare disease. I couldn't be in physical contact with anyone. A thick glass imprisoned me from the rest of the world. Before I entered, my mother gave me a rag doll that I held constantly for five years while in medical confinement." Jodie, sobbing, continued. "My doll disintegrated after a few years, and I was left with nothing to touch or love in the facility."

I was heartbroken for her. The other thirty-nine students leaned forward in silent support as I held the young woman in my arms until she was ready to let go. Her willingness to release control and risk being seen for exactly who she was set the tone for the rest of the week in my class. Everyone took at least small steps outside of their neutral, safe existence. They took the chance to release the need to control, and the power in the room was undeniable.

I was sad to hear from another student that, six months later, Jodie died. The debilitating illness of her childhood had taken its toll. However, it lifted my sense of purpose to also find out that her last months on earth were lived with confidence, self-acceptance, and appreciation for what made her unique. It was her courage to be vulnerable that allowed her to trust others and live a life of dignity. Her experience in my class was profound for everyone in the room. I will always be grateful to her, as she reminded me, once again, that we are all the same.

I am a top Hollywood acting coach who teaches actors to open up, let go, and create a more fulfilling life on stage or on camera, and even more important, in real life.

Actors, at any age, are just like all of us. They believe if they can control their results and book jobs, they will be happy. It's a myth. Control is our nemesis. Control builds a wall. Control protects us from everything, including our own feelings, even joy. And this need to control is a universal theme for human beings. We've been led to believe that being in control is the way to a successful and happy life.

How's it going for you so far?

I thought so.

It's time to challenge that belief system and find some real joy.

CONTROL DOES ONE THING REALLY WELL: IT GETS IN YOUR WAY

Now, this control thing is sneaky. It hides behind many different masks.

I always thought it was my wife (yes, I have a wife) who was the controlling one. Susan controls the volume on the remote. She drives the car, even if I am in the driver's seat! At a restaurant, she always has to sit facing the people, leaving me to face the bathroom door. She is a neat freak. I can come home from a day of work only to find that half my clothes in the closet aren't there anymore. She declutters everything. It's not unusual to find my hearing aid in the garbage!

But then, I looked closer at myself. It seems there's more than one control freak living at our address. I freak out if we are five minutes late. I demand to take thousands of pictures of my son, Michael, even though he has forbidden it. I even control how my friends play charades!

CONTROL IS THE ENEMY, STRUCTURE IS THE HERO

Structure is a map, a guide, and a frame that allows us some freedom to be messy inside. What would happen if I applied some structure and dropped the control? Even if I'm ten minutes late, I need to drive like I am early, stay calm, take some breaths, and realize there will be no consequences. Maybe I don't get to take all the pictures I want of my son. Maybe I can just live in the memory of those moments and ask for one or two that represents our time together. And maybe, just maybe, I can share with others the structure of the game by allowing them to play it their own way. Wow—giving up control is so much less stressful!

POUND FOR POUND, STRUCTURE MEASURES UP

After a year of eating whatever I wanted, I was informed by my jeans that it was time to return to Weight Watchers (now known as WW International), which I had used twenty years earlier to drop weight. Today's Weight Watchers is a whole different program with many new, complicated (for me, anyway) choices—instead of counting calories, every food is assigned a number of points. There's so much more room for eating a lot more food. It scared me in the beginning. I didn't trust it. I controlled everything that I put in my mouth. I stuck to eating only the "zero point" foods. Everyone told me that I could eat the daily chocolate See's lollipop that I love because it was "only" four points. Four points! That's a quarter of my allowance for a day!

After my first week on the program, I went to a party for a film that I had worked on. All the drinks and food were free, so I didn't even think about what I was about to put in my mouth. I was offered a cosmo and took my first sip. Then it occurred to me. Weight Watchers! I nonchalantly placed the drink on a corner table (cosmos are notoriously high in points). All around me were plates of greasy hamburgers, fatty spare ribs, and spicy french fries. I started to panic. Would I lose control? What should I do?

I didn't need to control it. I only needed some structure. I went home and ate a turkey sandwich with cheese and mustard and sliced apples in place of bread—delicious, and one point! By replacing control with structure, I can have a cosmo as long as I made a conscious decision. I can keep my chocolate lollipop in my daily routine. I can choose to eat steak and not a side of beef. I can eat a baked potato without it dripping in butter and scoops of sour cream. It was a liberating experience to know I can trust my choices within a structure. Every choice was a small victory that came with happiness.

A DREADED SPEECH,
SAVED BY STRUCTURE

One afternoon, I got a call from Robert, a top executive at a prestigious bank. "I was told you were the person who could make me a better speaker. I don't seem to have a knack for it."

On the first day, when he arrived at my studio, I realized we had a lot of work to do. He was sternly dressed in a pinstripe suit, a skinny tie, and recently polished shoes. It all looked like it came from my father's closet. Emotionless, with a frown on his face, he pulled out his typed pages and started reciting the speech: the mission of Wells Fargo and how to satisfy customers' needs. He had every fact listed, accompanied by the most boring slides.

I stopped him halfway through. I suggested we let go of the facts and 90 percent of the slides. He told me that he needed all of it so he could know exactly what he was doing. I asked him to trust me and let go of control.

I had him get up and talk about the things he loved and the people he felt passionate about. At first, he resisted, thinking it was not about the speech, but he went with it. Next, I had him talk about the company and the best day he ever spent there. His stern face softened, and his frown turned upside down. Eventually, I helped him understand that there is no such thing as a "speech." He could let go of his choices by replacing control with structure. He could frame what he wanted to say but not be controlled by every word. I encouraged him to use this structure to become a messy human being and to trust that his relationship with the audience would guide him.

By the third session, Robert wore a casual shirt. The following week, he exchanged his suit for jeans, a sweater, and a pair of Nike Air sneakers. Later, he dared to replace his Honda with a BMW! It was a huge victory for this courageous young man. Robert left not only as a better communicator but a happier person.

OH GOD, I NEED THIS JOB!

Do you freak out over the interview process? If so, you are not alone. Many people dread it. They spend hours deciding what clothes to wear. Some come up with a biography to memorize. They know every word they are going to say and, therefore, assume they will be in control of the interview. Others spend days researching the company to know precisely what the interviewer wants when they walk into the room. They can't stop obsessing about how to control the interview in order to land the job.

Believe me, I understand how scary interviews can be. When I wrote my first book, *How to Get the Part . . . Without Falling Apart!,* my publisher booked me on CNN and *Entertainment Tonight.* I was freaking out! I was sure only a handful of people would be watching, but I was scared shitless! I was sitting on a tall stool in a small studio, waiting to be interviewed, when the panic and racing thoughts began. *What are they going to ask me? Will I be good? Will I throw up?*

I started to get palpitations. I noticed the interviewer looking behind me. I turned around and saw someone holding up a board with questions written in pencil. (That's how low-budget this show was.) *Holy shit! I don't know any of those answers!* I screamed inside my head. I felt faint and couldn't breathe, but right before I was sure that I was going to pass out, I asked myself, *What would Margie Haber do?*

My answer was, Margie would let go of control by putting the attention on the other person.

So, I looked at this interviewer who was putting on ruby lipstick, using the camera lens as a mirror. It was then that it came to me. She needs my help! I started feeling empathetic and shifted the attention from my concerns to help her have a good interview. Within that structure, all my fear and my need to control dissipated. I was able to communicate and enjoy the interview. What a relief!

Success is a beast. And it actually puts the emphasis on the wrong thing. You get away with more instead of looking in.

—Brad Pitt, actor and film producer

✳ Embrace Your Imperfections ✳

MISTAKES ARE YOUR FRIENDS

Mistakes take you off autopilot and make you human. Ironically, we are all terrified of making a mistake, but it is our mistakes that allow us to grow, be creative, and be happy. It's our imperfections that are fascinating. Perfectionism is contagious and a soul-crushing pursuit. Our society rewards us for our achievements but does it ever reward us for the journey? We have a compulsive need to achieve our goals. Devastation occurs when we don't get it right. Actors are always striving for perfection. They are not happy unless they have every word memorized, every moment controlled by what they think the casting director wants. So, they walk into the audition afraid of being imperfect, and by doing so, they rob themselves of their greatest strengths—the flaws that make them human. That is their magic, which is the crack of their creativity.

Aidan Whytock's Story— Stuttering with Freedom

started stammering at five years old. It had a huge impact on my confidence. Sadly and obviously, bullying came part and parcel with it. I've been picked on, ganged up on, hit, and beaten. I withdrew. I avoided any situation where things could go wrong.

Stuttering is the reason I got into acting. At boarding school, they were auditioning for the school play. The idea of being on stage appealed to me, but the possibility of stammering in front of an audience was paralyzing. My dear old dad, the wise man that he is, encouraged me to face my fears. I auditioned and got the part. I rehearsed my one line (I believe the line was, "Yes, it's over there.") for weeks. Finally, the night of the show arrived. I still recall standing in the wings. The moment was upon me: I walked out onto the stage, waited for my cue, and hit the line. The audience erupted in laughter, but this time, not at me—with me. My line was the punch line of the gag. Never have I felt so alive.

The fear of stammering in casting sessions was petrifying. I've learned ways around it, but it has been stressful and exhausting.

Then I started working with Margie, who told me that she wanted me to stutter in class. She didn't want me to control it, quite the opposite. I had to use the words that were written, not replace them with words that were easier for me to say.

"You can be imperfect," Margie reminded me. "We all are. Fifty percent of stuttering is the fear that you will stutter. Give yourself permission, and it will relieve the pressure." For the first time in my life, I was free from controlling the way I talked. Imperfection is liberating!

YOU WERE BORN PERFECT. YOU DON'T HAVE TO STRIVE FOR IT

A theatrical manager called me to see if I could work with a young boy who was cast in the Broadway production of *Les Misérables*. At my studio, his mother warned him while straightening out his tie and combing his hair: "Remember to shake Mrs. Haber's hand. Be polite and listen."

The seven-year-old boy stretched out his hand to shake mine, saying, "It is a pleasure to meet you."

Instead of taking his hand, I pulled him onto my lap and tickled him until he laughed so hard that it released his playfulness. The iron grip of control and the pressure to be a good little boy dropped away. After one session, he was full of wide-eyed curiosity and enthusiasm. His real self came to life . . . and so did the role he played on stage. It was a victory.

When I was a little kid, I easily went from playing a cowgirl like Dale Evans (Roy Rogers's partner) and eating cans of cold beans, all suited up with my six-shooters, to just hanging out with my sisters and my beautiful mom, while she was laying in the hammock. I wasn't trying to control the moment or determine the future. I was free to laugh, cry, sing, and dance. I only lived in the present.

We can let go of control when we stop thinking about ourselves.

RELATIONSHIP OVERCOMES FEAR

My good friend Neil's memorial service in 2014 was at UCLA in a theater that held a thousand people. He was a well-known and loved agent who died of ALS. Five people were asked to speak at his service, and I was one of them. I accepted, but regretted that decision every second before the memorial. I spent endless, sleepless nights writing and rewriting the speech. I am always terrified of not living up to what is expected of me and afraid that I will not do a great job. When the memorial service began, I sacrificed being in the now, listening to other eulogies and enjoying the process, as I sat rereading the words of my speech over and over. When it was my turn, I climbed the stairs of the stage as if I were going to my execution. I felt I had to be perfect, or else I would disappoint everyone and embarrass myself. There was a moment where I thought my best move would be to turn around and escape, but when I heard my name, I timidly appeared on stage. On the screen behind me was a video of Neil in his wheelchair, laughing as he told one of his hilarious jokes. At that moment, I looked at him and said, "This is for you, my friend." I turned around, facing the standing-room-only crowd. I felt my power surging back. Letting go of control and making my relationship with Neil more important than my fear saved the day.

Haddis Tadesse's Story— My Pursuit of Excellence

Those who know me well will attest to my commitment to excellence in my professional and personal life. And it's in applying that same commitment to explore acting that led me to Margie, at the recommendation of those I admire in the industry.

For well over twenty years, I have been shaped by my career in the political and development space and highly value the currency of success in a capricious global environment. I am trained and excel at making decisions fast, with great conviction, and do so consistently. I applied the tools and approaches that served me well in this new acting endeavor. I came into each coaching session with Margie having prepared thoroughly, making sure everything was planned to perfection. But here, in this new world, in front of cameras and an industry giant looking over me, I was completely out of my element and experienced a new challenge.

Session after session, I came prepared, yet I still felt inadequate. I wanted to be in total control. I had the erroneous belief that my approach in the corporate world of accepting nothing less than perfection would serve me. One day in the middle of class, in front of everyone, something foreign to me occurred. Despite my greatest attempts to hide it, I broke down at the possibility of failure and disappointment.

It is in these crucial moments that great coaches recognize and maximize such teachable moments. Margie dropped everything and fully consumed herself in the moment. She listened thoughtfully to how I felt and why, asked honest questions, and started to guide me into sharing why I was so afraid of being less than perfect.

I realized that demanding perfection could also bring unhappiness. I learned to embrace imperfections. Being perfect isn't the goal. Now that I am slowly getting back to my love for the arts, the experience with Margie was inspiring. I went to Margie to satisfy my curiosity about acting but came out having also gained meaningful life lessons. It is okay to be vulnerable and to let go of control. After all, it is so human.

—Haddis D. Tadesse, Director, Ethiopia,
Bill & Melinda Gates Foundation

*Perfection is not just about control.
It's also about letting go. Surprise yourself
so you can surprise the audience.*

—Thomas Leroy, fictional character in the movie *Black Swan*,
screenplay by Mark Heyman, John McLaughlin, and Andres Heinz

MARGISM: F*CK PERFECTIONISM

Instead of striving for perfection, strive for flexibility. The mindset of flexibility allows us to live in the unknown. We can release control in the flexibility provided by structure. So many beautiful surprises can fill us up in our journey when we take the chance to accept that being human means being imperfect.

- Instead of being afraid of living in the unknown, I live in it.

- Instead of striving for perfection, I embrace imperfections.
- Instead of freaking out that I may make mistakes, I remind myself that mistakes are my friends.

I've been absolutely terrified every minute of my life—and I've never let it keep me from doing a single thing I wanted to do.

—Georgia O'Keeffe, artist

Studio Focus: Conversations from the Classroom
STUMBLING INTO SOMETHING BEAUTIFUL

INT. CLASSROOM—DAY
MARGIE speaks to Adam, who's just finished reading a cold slice (scene) from The Morning Show.

MARGIE

So, Adam, there are different ways of controlling and different ways of letting go of control. Let's say you go into the audition knowing what you want to do, but then something happens—the phrasing goes off or you don't remember your line. And panic occurs, so you close off to protect yourself. When you and I were just talking, you were "light" about it, and it made you more vulnerable; it brightened you up. What's interesting to me is the way we can release control. One of the beautiful ways is with joy. When you were talking right now, you were releasing it with joy, but when you were doing the slice, you fell back into your bad habit. That's what humans do. Did you feel angry with yourself?

ADAM

I felt like I was just stumbling through it.

MARGIE

But when you were stumbling through it, what was your experience of it?

ADAM

Well, it wasn't joy—

MARGIE

Exactly!

The class laughs with her.

So, what's the opposite of joy?

ADAM

In a cowering tone.

Not joy—

MARGIE

Not joy.

She turns to the class.

What's a good opposite word for joy?

Margie, repeating suggestions from the group—

Frustration. Misery. Despair.

  Angry, negative—so, what happens, Adam, is that even now when you say, "I can tell you it wasn't joy," you were joyful! It was a beautiful mask. Yet, even masks can have some vulnerability. The mask you used during the slice was not joyful and did not allow you to be vulnerable.

ADAM

That's a light-bulb moment for me. I am so afraid to catch myself acting. I wanted to feel my way through the whole thing so it would be authentic.

MARGIE

So, what could you do when that happens?

ADAM

I could just let it go and play with what's happening in the moment. Stumble around in a place of happiness instead of a place of "What the fuck is going on here."

MARGIE

Enjoy the stumble. You're going to stumble. In life, we stumble all the time. And for whatever reason, we have this erroneous belief that stumbling is bad. Until we can get into our soul that stumbling actually propels us into something beautiful, we're always going to keep that desire to control so that we feel we're doing a good thing. And it's tough.

> *People call these things imperfections, but they're not. Ah, that's the good stuff.*
>
> —Sean Maguire, fictional character in the movie *Good Will Hunting*; screenplay by Matt Damon and Ben Affleck

FORGET THE SUPERSIZE, SMALL VICTORIES RULE!

A flag doesn't reach the top of a steel pole with one swift pull of the rope. You are the flag, and the rope on the pulley is your journey. The rope must drop lower and descend temporarily to raise the flag higher and then higher. There is no upward movement without the opposite. We have times of setbacks, introspection, and reassessing the person we are becoming. It's how we learn and change through small victories that give us more insight and confidence to become the lead in our individual lives. Eventually, you will get there.

* Letting Go *

REROUTE YOUR LIFE MAP

The only way to remove control from your life is to let go. I can't control everyone's life. I can't even control my own. We can only do the best we can and let the universe take over from there. It's acceptance that frees us.

I had a plan in place for what my life was going to be. I had decided that I would marry, be a mother of three bright children, a famous actress and singer, and I would live happily ever after.

I was hanging on to that life plan and was totally controlled by it. Then, in my early twenties, when I understood that I am a gay woman, I was horrified that I wasn't going to have the picture-perfect image I had created.

I went to a fabulous therapist, Betty Berzon, who asked me to describe the picture I saw in my head. I described it all, including a house with a picket fence and a successful husband.

She didn't see a problem with my vision. Instead, she made me understand that I could have that picture if I replaced the husband with a woman (at that time, in the 1970s, there was no such thing as gay marriage). It was like a light bulb went on, and I could see a new, beautiful image of what my future could be with a child and a loved one.

The same was true for my career. When I let go of the picture of being a famous actress and singer, I found this incredible career that I would never have discovered if I had stayed in my controlled vision of success. I truly have the best life because of my willingness to let go. I learned that I could let go and not lose anything.

Studio Focus: **Conversations from the Classroom**
OH, SHIT! I'M GOING TO CRASH!

INT. CLASSROOM—DAY

MARGIE

So, what's interesting about control is that when you know you are doing well, and everything is going along smoothly, you feel real confident and cool. But when things are going badly, you feel you have to control it. Then, the control injures you. It becomes a vicious cycle. So, it feels like it's a matter of life and death, instead of letting go and saying: "Well, I screwed up, but so what? I'm going to have fun with it." It's not heart surgery; it's only human behavior.

R.D., when you think you are in control, do you actually feel that you are out of control?

R.D.

I mean, I have my entire life. I definitely think I have to get back on that road.

MARGIE

And what will happen if you are not on that road?

R.D.

I'm going to crash.

MARGIE

You are going to crash. And that is terrifying.

R.D.

Yes, I am terrified of that crash.

MARGIE

Here's the truth. We are all terrified of crashing. But what is fascinating is that when you do crash, you survive. We just don't believe it. Our worry isn't anything more than a bad habit. We believe that if we keep control of our lives, we will be all right.

But when things go wrong, you have to know it's just an opportunity to learn, forgive yourself, and have fun with it.

Ernest Hemingway gave

this advice to an aspiring writer:

"Out of every ten stories I write, only one is

any good and I throw the other nine away."

I'M HAVING A HEART ATTACK.
OR IS IT A PANIC ATTACK?

I adopted my son, Michael. It was the most wonderful time of my life and the most frightening. I had to do it all on my own. I had no partner at that time and couldn't use the usual channels to adopt a baby.

I placed ads in many newspapers throughout the United States, installed a red phone, and waited for the calls.

A seventeen-year-old girl, who said she didn't want her mother to raise her child, seemed like the perfect match. We agreed to have her come out to California until she delivered the baby. I kept telling everyone I knew that I was in total control. It was exciting, and I didn't want to look at my fear. Then, a week before the birth mother's arrival in Los Angeles, I woke up with shortness of breath. I was hyperventilating and got very dizzy. I tried to walk, but the world started spinning. I couldn't see objects in my peripheral vision. I felt tingling and tightening in my chest and pain going down my arm. Nausea came over me as I started sweating profusely and dry heaving. I couldn't breathe.

Somehow, I made it to my phone and called my doctor. She thought it sounded more like a panic attack. She had me breathe into a brown paper bag to regulate my breath and then to visualize calm ocean waves. I started to come back to myself.

After that episode, I went to the UCLA Anxiety Disorders Clinic and learned what caused my panic attack. I was so afraid to be out of control with this big life change of becoming a mom that I was holding on too tight to the ledge. I was too afraid to let go. For a year, I had to learn to let myself have panic attacks. I had to prove that I would survive through the temporary discomfort. As I let go of controlling them, they became less frequent and less intense. It was the "letting go" that freed me from my terror.

> *It feels like I've been thrown down a chute.*
> *I'm careening forward, trying not to get too*
> *banged up, utterly out of control of my*
> *descent, and somewhere in the dark, there's*
> *a hole waiting for me to fall through it.*

—Laura McBride, author, *We Are Called to Rise*

Richard Gunn's Story— Filming *Clemency*

I found out a little less than a week before filming began that I'd booked a lead in a feature, *Clemency*, opposite an absolute powerhouse of an actress, Alfre Woodard. I was elated and frankly a bit panicked—how was I supposed to prepare in time? I was to play a deputy warden to Alfre's warden of a death row prison. Heavy, poignant subject matter—a deeply emotional story. I'd just have to do the best I could with that short time, but being someone who likes to prepare, I was already fearful.

I kept reminding myself that I needed to let go of control, but I didn't have time to take a breath. I received the shoot schedule. Guess what? First up, a "slice of life" where my character gets into it with Alfre's character about the way she's running the prison—quite a heated moment between the two of us in front of other members of the prison staff. This would be my first scene on my very first day.

It was a new set with new people, no rehearsals, and I had to hit the ground in full tilt—hair, makeup, and wardrobe, not to mention signing contracts along with other bureaucratic endeavors that can be really distracting. Compartmentalization is a key skill here. So, I get up well before dawn—fortunately, I left two and a half hours in advance—Los Angeles traffic can be devastating, and being late just is another control issue for me

Then began the wait in my trailer until I was called to set. I admit, at this point, fear is taking over. I'm biting my nails while going over my lines. Hydrating. Mulling over the future that was very soon to come. Flashing through my mind were fearful questions. *What will Alfre be like? How about the others? What does the set even look like?* I needed some answers to find some way of being in control.

A knock on my door, and a pleasant PA said, "Mr. Gunn, are you ready to head to set?"

Ready? Seriously? We were filming in an actual prison near downtown Los Angeles—defunct, but the energy in the place was palpable, crushing. After arriving on set, I met the talented star Alfre Woodard—professional, gracious, and just as powerful in real life as she is on-screen. My god, this woman has presence, and I'm about to go up against her. (So, I have a professional crush on her—so what?) At this point, I'm thinking I'd be happy just to hold my own. We sit down, run through the scene, feeling out the blocking, and so on, and . . . we're off.

Looking back on this, I realize that anxiety, that fear bubbling in my veins, was a gift. A gift to accept—a yes, thank you—to be used, pulled in, and harnessed into the duality of the character and myself. But I was so busy trying to shove it down, "be confident," that I missed much of the joyful experience.

I scolded myself. *You have nothing to fear*. But the fear just belly laughed in my face. It was about being perfect, about getting it right that was getting in my way. I would so like to go back and revel in that fear. It was indeed a gift—a magical gift, ripe for the plucking, but my grip was holding it too tight.

My new mantra: Fear is my best friend. Just let go.

When I let go of what I am,

I become what I might be.

—Lao Tzu, Chinese philosopher and founder of Taoism

* Right Is Wrong *

THE FREEWAY WAS A GHOST TOWN

What is it about human beings that we think being right will make us happy? Right is another way to control a conversation and win. Is winning worth it? I know even in the littlest things, I love to be right. As I stated before, I am a control freak when it comes to time. I have to be on time, or I feel out of control. The combination of wanting to be right and being on time can be problematic. I remember one incident, in 1969, when my best friend, Mary Wilson, was in New York City. She was in a group called the Supremes. They were Motown's number one female group with many hit songs and international fame.

The group was scheduled to perform at the Westbury Music Fair (now known as the NYCB Theatre at Westbury) on Long Island, and we needed to drive from Manhattan on a Friday to get there. Anyone who lives in New York City knows how insane traffic can be going to

Long Island. I was from there, so I knew it would take forever if we left after 2:00 p.m. When I was with Mary and the rest of the group the night before, I suggested they leave early the next day to avoid the gridlock. Diana Ross disagreed and we proceeded to leave much later that day.

In the limo on the way to the gig, I am ashamed to admit, I was praying that we would be stuck in bottleneck traffic so I could be right. I did feel "Jewish guilt" in thinking that, but nothing was more important to me than winning. Maybe it was karma or maybe it was a coincidence but, for whatever reason, the freeway was like a ghost town—practically no one was on it. We got to the theater in forty-five minutes. Diana had triumphed! She won. I lost. After that incident, I saw a mirror reflection of myself that I didn't like. Being right doesn't look good.

Bad habits are hard to break. Bringing up my son, it was always important to me that he knew I was right and he was wrong. Now he does the same thing to me! It's like a temporary high. It feels really good for that moment, but it doesn't last long. When we believe that we are right and the other person is wrong, we ignore our own problems and focus on that person's problems. Little do we know how destructive that behavior is.

Johnno Wilson's Story— I Follow the Rules

am a control junkie. Like many of us, I grew up wanting to "do well." I wanted to excel academically and athletically, and I wanted my parents to be proud of me. And I accomplished that. I followed the rules (for the most part), took leadership positions at school, got on the honor roll, was the captain of my football teams, and that was all well and good, but it also instilled in me a need to be "right," to do whatever I was doing the "right" way. Now, that is something I'm working on letting go in my work with Margie.

There is a subtle balance to everything we do. The need to do well is great, because it pushes me to be professional, work hard, and make sure I'm living life and creating. When I have opportunities to audition or film something, it keeps me diligent. But wanting to be "right" gets in the way of embracing my imperfections and using pieces of myself, which, in turn, hinders my ability to play, which is something I love to do, and frankly, I'm pretty good at it.

Usually, it takes the "frozen read exercise" in class to let go and play with my idea. Margie gives us a scene, or a "slice" as she calls it, with no time to look it over before performing it. So, here I am, trying to decide what to do with it. But when I let go of that need to know everything, I'm able to forget about my preplanned stuff. I've loosened up because my need to be right has been tossed out the window, and I can zone in on the other person. All of a sudden, the words don't matter as much. I feel more comfortable in the space and body, and I begin to listen and let it affect me.

This exercise helps me to remember that I need to embrace my imperfect life. People on the other side of the camera want to see me. They want to see an authentic, imperfect person living an authentic, imperfect life. It's a work in progress, but I'm beginning to learn that the "right" way to do things is to let go of control and the need to be right. It's embracing all of my imperfections, playfulness, and essence, trusting that I am enough.

⁎ The Power of Silence ⁎

THERAPY SESSION—EXECUTIVE FUNCTION, CONTROLLING THE CHATTER

MARGIE

I find it difficult to stay in silence. I feel more in control when I'm talking.

THERAPIST

Be intentional about it. Let go of control and find peace.

MARGIE

My mind is trying to be in control, and I need to let go of that control.

THERAPIST

Telling yourself to stop thinking doesn't work. When the chattering is out of control, and you can't stop thinking, it's the observation of your breath that will stop the drip, drip, dripping of the faucet of endless thoughts in your head.

MARGIE

At this moment, I can observe my heart beating, my brain obsessing, or my emotions getting out of control. It's the observation that allows me to find quiet.

THERAPIST

There you go. Don't make it good or bad. I am talking about balance. We all have cognitive skills, our executive function, so we can operate daily as an adult and a human. You could get out of executive function by simply washing the dishes while really paying attention to each dish in your hand.

MARGIE

Mindfully doing the dishes, taking walks, and eating slowly all allow me to be silent. We don't sit still long enough to let intuition come to the forefront. I can create some space for quiet to allow my intuition to be heard.

THERAPIST

Then, you can live in silence and let go of your control.

*　　*　　*

Studio Focus: **Conversations from the Classroom**
TAP DANCING

Many of us are afraid to stop talking. I have been known to be one of them. I sometimes forget to take a breath and, certainly, have forgotten the power of silence.

INT. CLASSROOM—DAY

MARGIE

Gosh, Jesse! You have succeeded beyond your wildest dreams of letting go of control. Today you did something great through the power of silence.

JESSE

It was uncomfortable to let go of control. I wanted to fill the space with something to do or more dialogue. I had to let go and trust that it was okay to not have something to say or do.

MARGIE

Actors can be afraid to allow for silence because we can't control the listener's reaction. Being silent feels vulnerable. We associate silence with being boring or bored, which creates fear. But silence is interesting, because it gets us out of our need to control.
To the class:
Let's talk about it. So, please fill the silence with your thoughts about the power of silence.
Class laughs.

JODY

It's filled with a lot of things underneath. It's beautiful to watch.

SARAH

The thoughts were there. There's energy. Even though she was silent, you could see them.

PETER

Her thoughts gave her power, because she didn't know which way she was going to go.

SAMMY

There was not one moment where she wasn't completely alive.

MARGIE

In life, people are so afraid of taking a pause, and that pause can be a moment of breath. But silence is longer, and it can be really intimidating. When we keep talking and talking and talking, it's like tap dancing. We keep going so that there is no room for anyone to say anything against us. Being silent is very vulnerable.

To Jesse:

The thing you did that was so great today is that you didn't just have thoughts. You took the time to have a silent conversation, which brought out your curiosity. *I don't want to say anything, but maybe I should. Oh, this is interesting. I think I want to find out more about him.* That silent, internal discussion takes you away from your own fear and puts you into the world of the other person. All sorts of interesting behavior occurred.

PATTI

They were almost building on each other.

MARGIE

And that's when we pay attention. If we, as human beings, were able to take a camera and do a close-up on what another person was actually thinking, we would be intrigued, wouldn't we? Give yourself permission to live in the world of silence. You deserve it. It's powerful.

✳ Acceptance ✳

GO WITH THE FLOW

Sometimes we have to walk through the fire and know we will be fine. Letting go is accepting. We are powerless over others. We can only take care of ourselves. If I accept that I am limited, then I will accept the limitations of another. Acceptance is the willingness to not have all the answers and to be okay with it. It is all about having realistic expectations of others and ourselves. We need to go with the flow and realize that what is supposed to happen will happen. If I am in acceptance, I can establish relationships without any expectations. I will forgive others and myself.

For after all, the best thing one can do
When it is raining, is to let it rain.

—Henry Wadsworth Longfellow, from
"The Poet's Tale: The Birds of Killingworth"

Some of the biggest failures
I ever had were successes.

—Pearl Bailey, from her 1971 memoir,
Talking to Myself

Annie Karstens's Story—
When He Flaps His Hands, I Flap Mine

When my son was diagnosed with autism at age two and a half, I felt more powerless than I ever had in my life. When someone tells you your child might not speak, might forever wildly flap his hands, will likely need around-the-clock care and may never have the social capability to form friendships—it's like a horse kick to the gut. Actually, for me, it was more like that horse took off in a frantic gallop while tied to a rope that I held in my bare hands. As that rope just tore out of my grip, with it went my sense of control, of personal power, of what I thought I knew about parenting.

What was left was grief. We had to grieve the loss of what we thought our son could do or could be as he grew up. I could do nothing to fix it, to cure it, to write a strongly worded letter to whoever was in charge.

I was pointed toward resources, therapies, special diets, genetic testing, biomedical approaches, and early intervention schools. I joined support groups, playgroups, counseling groups, homeopathic groups (really, the groups are endless). I filled my days (and still often do, to be fair) with educating myself and my husband on autism, its treatments and outcomes. All of the research and connection with other families gave me back a tiny bit of control, of hope that I could actually do something to make life for my boy as "normal" as possible. This pursuit of what-else-can-I-do kept me up at night, distracted me from my job and personal passions. My own identity was on permanent pause.

And yet it was my son who turned the lights back on for me. Regardless of my near-nuclear stress levels or steely determination to fix him—this little boy, in his relentless pursuit of love and play, began to fix me. His joy and his love for me were bigger than my fear. And the inevitable happened, because his sweet soul left me no other choice. I accepted him for exactly who he is.

That simple act of acceptance released me from the resentment of his autism diagnosis. It released me from the powerlessness I felt over having a child who was "abnormal" or "unwell." My own life came back into view. I am a good mom, a damn good mom. When he flaps his hands, I flap mine. When he wants to sing the same song over and over (and over), I sing along with him. I work with other moms of autistic kids to help them get through the trauma and find resources. We still do the research, therapies, and biomed interventions. But they don't rule my life and don't define my relationship with my son. For me, personal power came only after I accepted that I had no control over the outcome, and I embraced a full and total acceptance of my son, of autism, of our new normal. And that power keeps me present, keeps me focused on what matters. Love, it's a powerful thing.

Studio Focus: Conversations from the Classroom
"FUCK IT!" CONTROL JUST AIN'T WORTH IT!

INT. CLASSROOM—DAY

MARGIE
Lisa, I'm so excited to see your power today! It was beautiful. You are changing, no longer controlling—your body, your responses, what you say. What I see now is this beautiful, young, warm, open person.

LISA
I like it!

MARGIE

Is it true?

LISA

I have been working on just saying, "Fuck it," and having fun. If I try to control everything, it sucks all the joy out of it, so why the hell am I here?

MARGIE

And do you spend a lot of time trying to control people and yourself in your personal life?

LISA

(Laughs) My husband would say that I'm bossy. I have an oldest-daughter syndrome of thinking I have the answers. I have to take care of everyone. I am working on it in life and in my art.

MARGIE

Everyone is a control junkie. I was proud that you let yourself go. You trusted your inside beauty to come out. You brought your passion. Why would you diminish that part of you? Control just isn't worth it.

If you're offered a seat on a rocket ship,
don't ask what seat. Just get on.

—Sheryl Sandberg, chief operating officer, Facebook, recounting advice from Eric Schmidt, then chief executive officer, Google

POWER CHALLENGE

- Define the difference in your life between control and structure. Remember (structure allows us to loosen up and be spontaneous within a framework.)

- Where in your life would you benefit from embracing your imperfections?
- Was there a time when your insistence on being right injured a particular relationship? Write down an imaginary conversation with this person in which not needing to be right leads to a different outcome.
- Imagine giving a speech or going to a job interview. Write down four ways in which letting go of control and being spontaneous might actually lead to success in this endeavor.
- Have you ever been deeply stressed or had a full-on panic attack? Take a deep soothing inhale through the nose, let it out powerfully through the mouth, and smile. Describe the thoughts that changed during that exercise and what parts of your body relaxed afterward.
- When are you afraid of silence?
- List the ways you can let go of control and say, "Fuck it!"

2

Getting Out of Your Comfort Zone

* Ouch! It's Too Scary Out There! *

The word "risk" is on the cover of this book for a reason. We all have to risk stepping out of our comfort zone if we want to grow.

Most of us equate happiness with being comfortable and safe. We hang out with friends who offer no inspiration, stay in a job we don't love, eat the same foods, wear the same styles, and visit the same vacation spots. Some of us even remain in relationships that don't support us or are negative, because they feel familiar or comfortable.

We zone out in the comfort zone.

We are stuck in neutral, idling in place, not going anywhere.

How is it for you? Do you coast in neutral for way too long? Or perhaps, like me, you go from zero to 80 mph in sixty seconds. Both can be examples of a comfort zone.

* * *

Taylor Carter's Story—
First One on the Dance Floor

I feel like, for the majority of my life, I tend to remain in a comfort zone. If I have a job, I stick to it as long as possible, even if I hate it. I'm constantly living in fear—fear of the unknown, the what-ifs that hold me back tremendously. It takes me forever to make even a simple decision, let alone a life-changing one. I have to be sure all ends meet, and I'm doing the right thing for not only myself but for all parties involved. I feel it's easier not to be in a relationship and save myself the trouble of having to worry about another person. When I am in one, I stay stagnant because I don't want to cause harm or hurt to the other person, even if I feel I'm not getting anything out of it. I stay stuck in fear of losing that person for good, but I just end up losing myself, convincing myself that this is what's good for me because he or she is a good person or is good to me, or on paper we're good together, even if that's not how I really feel.

In my career, I see myself achieving so much. I see my wildest dreams coming true so vividly, but I end up holding myself back because of fear. Fear of the unknown can be paralyzing. I've known my whole life what I wanted to do. My family knew at a very young age that I was a "performer," but I doubted myself because it feels like it's almost impossible to get there, a one-in-a-million chance. This depressing state has become my comfort zone, and I am working hard to get out of it.

Now, I'm learning how to get out of the comfort zone:

I'm forcing myself into new situations with new people or strangers. Even if I have to fake the confidence, it's easier to fake it with strangers because there's nothing to lose. I have no choice but to live in that present moment and adapt to the environment around me, usually by being the first one on the dance floor. Sometimes I like to play my favorite music and dance down the street, knowing everyone is watching this crazy girl dance her way through life.

For people like Taylor, moving out of the comfort zone means taking a risk to become more visible.

For others, like myself, the comfort zone is making a grand entrance, doing everything big, and taking up too much space. This behavior stems from my childhood as the youngest in my family and wanting to be noticed. I would entertain, talk really fast to get a word in, or behave inappropriately simply to be seen. I got what I wanted and have chased it ever since. Negative attention for me was better than no attention at all. When I go to a party, I like to become the center of attention, even knowing that it might backfire and I might be criticized. The fear of being invisible has haunted me my entire life.

> *I have to be visible or else*
> *I would be miserable.*
>
> —Anonymous

Every day, I have to remind myself to get out of my comfort zone in a way that brings happiness and is not forced out of my own fear.

I went to the premiere of the movie *Frankie & Alice*, in which my student, Halle Berry, plays the lead. I had not seen her for a while and was excited to tell her how much I loved her creation of this character. I wanted to run over and give her a big hug right away. Then, I remembered I had been working on a new method for myself called S-T-O-P, developed by Jon Kabat-Zinn, a prominent mindfulness researcher, as a way to step out of my comfort zone.

I stopped. I took a breath and observed that Halle was busy talking to other people. When there was a pause in their conversation, I proceeded to go over to her. We were delighted to see each other. Halle gave me the biggest hug, and we had a wonderful conversation. I have learned to use S-T-O-P in many parts of my life. This is a giant accomplishment for Margie Haber!

MARGISM: S-T-O-P

STOP

TAKE A BREATH

OBSERVE

PROCEED

On a busy teaching day, I might have only a few seconds to share something with my office manager. I used to barge into the office without noticing if anyone was on the phone. After all, *I'm the Boss Lady!* Now, even when I'm in a hurry, I apply S-T-O-P. It requires being present and a willingness to break a bad habit. Sometimes I am in such a rush that my feet can't keep up with my upper body as I plow forward to reach my destination. My nephew Barry loves to imitate this comical pace of mine.

I'M COMFORTABLE IN MY PRISON CELL

Bad habits keep us comfortable. We often see them as part of our family.

You might think, *I don't want to fight my relatives. I'm comfortable with them. They feel normal to me. They're my family. Why do I have to fight them?*

The answer is that bad habits are a prison. They're the bars of a cell, and I want you free, not zoned out in a cell of bad habits. I know they're ingrained, because you grew up with them, but you still have to cut them out of your life.

* Waiting for Permission— Coasting Under the Radar *

Bryce Lourie's Story— Worthy of My Space

My comfort zone is neutral. When I am unsure, I do less and stay where it is "safe." I do this in my life and in my acting. I am uncomfortable sharing my successes and strengths. I am always quick to diminish what I do and apologize for it.

One thing Margie said the other day in class that really stuck with me was, "You get what you put out." When I put out neutrality, safety, or caution, I have already taken away any opportunity to get anything creative or significant back.

What helps me overcome this is saying "fuck it." My need has to be more important than my fear. I have found that when my need is there, my creativity and trust in myself are much stronger than I think they are. I'm funny, I'm specific, I'm engaging, and I'm having fun.

I have plenty of creativity and life and fullness inside of me, but I give up my power and end up giving all of that good stuff away with it. Right now I'm working on believing that I am worthy of the space I take up and learning to be proud of it. My goal is not to be right, but to be full.

Take chances, make mistakes. That's how you grow. Pain nourishes your courage. You have to fail in order to practice being brave.

—Mary Tyler Moore, actress

Studio Focus: **Conversations from the Classroom**
HELP ME! I'M SHRINKING!

INT. CLASSROOM–DAY

NERIDA
I make myself smaller through self-deprecation. It's to make other people feel comfortable. Especially in an environment where I might be meeting new people or even just starting this class for the first time. I'll miniaturize myself, and I'm already very little.
She points to herself.
I make a joke about how insecure I am, which is true—I am. It's comforting to other people, because I come across as nonthreatening.

MARGIE
That keeps you safe.

NERIDA
I don't own my space. I can talk to anyone and relate to anyone about most things. I pride myself on that. I can have the conversation, but only by making a joke or putting myself down to ease their comfort.

MARGIE
That's also part of your comfort zone. Keeps you in neutral, which protects you from being seen. Putting yourself down allows you to stay in your "inferior" experience.

NERIDA

That's a problem when I need to impress someone in an audition, an interview, anything. I need to throw that away at those times. It's a cultural thing, too. You're the poppy that grows above, metaphorically speaking. Australians and Brits do it, too. They have this habit of cutting off the heads of all the tall poppies.

The class reacts in whispered wows.

MARGIE

We need to validate ourselves. What is the cure for shrinking? One way that works for me is to take a risk and help the person in front of me. I get empathetic and curious about that person. It erases my narcissistic worries about the impression I'm making. It's the relationship that allows us to get out of our own quicksand.

Jenny shares her perspective.

JENNY

I often minimize. As a six-foot-two female, there's a stereotype that comes along with me just being me. I've had people say they're intimidated by me. So, I become malleable. What I'm learning to do, instead of shrinking, is to rise to the occasion. I'm a teacher. I project the traits of being intelligent, worthy, and reliable. My students no longer see a towering presence, but a highly competent and compassionate human being.

Sterling Hawkins's Story— The Way Out Is Through

Three years ago, my life fell apart. My business failed. I had some family issues. My girlfriend broke up with me. And I mean, all of that's bad, right? But the worst part was the anxiety that went with it. I'm in my midthirties, and I'm a failure. There were dark times when I ran out of cash and slept in my parents' house. I thought: *I need to go back to my parents, who will save me, and I'll hopefully fade from existence, and nobody will remember me.* That was the kind of space I was in.

I isolated and retreated, because of the embarrassment and anxiety. My comfort zone was to stay alone and just hide from people. But I'm sitting at the computer one day, and you know how you get like hundreds of conference emails, where they invite you to a conference? "Join us here, spend $90, be an attendee." I got one of these. It was a conference in Singapore saying, "In six months, join us at this conference, pay $50, be an attendee."

My mom hadn't said it recently, but when I was a kid, I remember her saying, "The best way out is always through." It's actually a Robert Frost quote.

This just popped into my mind as I'm looking at the email and I'm thinking: *Maybe the way out is through. Maybe what I need to do right now is the thing that I'm literally most scared to do, which is to speak in front of people, show up with who and what I am.*

I hit the reply button and I wrote: "Why don't you have me speak? Best, Sterling." Which is insane. Nobody would expect to hear back from that.

Maybe it was luck, maybe the stars aligned, but the conference director gets back to me. Long story short, I ended up talking to him on the phone, and he exclaimed, "Yeah, I love what you're talking about."

I didn't have anything to lose. So, I said this thing that was way outside of my comfort zone. "What's your budget for speakers?" I had heard people got paid to speak, I knew it was a thing. And he actually gave me a number, and I replied, "I'd like to get paid double that."

He ended up emailing me a couple days later, and he said, "Okay, I'll fly you business class, and I'll meet you in the middle for the price."

And I'm smiling to myself, *I think I pushed this hard enough.*

I spent literally the next five months preparing like a crazy person. Because I've got anxiety, I created decks and I wrote scripts and then I did it all over again. And I practiced and practiced and practiced. I'm in my comfort zone when I'm prepared."

That was the theory anyway. But it didn't work because I started panicking about it. I couldn't sleep. I couldn't think straight. "Okay, if I memorize this thing cold, I'll be in better shape."

My friend/mentor Margie advised me not to focus on memorizing. She had this phrase technique of using the paper as part of your behavior. Margie assured me it's okay to be imperfect and to live in the unknown, but I was too set in my bad habits to let go of them.

The day comes, and I'm shaking, and I'm all flushed. I'm short of breath getting on the airplane.

I get there and do a quick rehearsal. It's big. It's a big auditorium, big stage, cameras in the back, big screens. I'm watching some of the other speakers, thinking: *I'm not good enough for this. I pulled the wool over somebody's eyes.* As it's leading up to me, I'm sweating. Thankfully, I'm wearing a suit, and it holds all the sweat that's pouring from my body. When I got up there, I don't remember most of it, but I delivered what the conference director told me was the best talk he's seen in seventeen years doing it!

The conference director put me in touch with all of his conference director friends. And all of a sudden I had a speaking career out of nothing. Here's the thing. I wish I had talked to Margie earlier. I would have saved myself an enormous amount of anxiety and would have had her tools for finding my personal power at my fingertips. Margie is an extraordinary, evolved person.

But I was lucky to have another woman guide me to be the best Sterling—my mom. "The way out is through."

I did the thing that I was most uncomfortable doing. I stepped out of my comfort zone.

You never change your life until you
step out of your comfort zone; change
begins at the end of your comfort zone.

—Roy T. Bennett, author, *The Light in the Heart*

HIDING OUT IN OUR COMFORT ZONE

"Please don't notice me."

"If I don't say anything, if I don't make waves, if I stay really quiet and take up very little space, then I will be safe from danger or pain."

"I'm not going to risk being humiliated by anyone."

These are all the thoughts of the inner child who is fearful, a part of each of us. How we respond to the fearful thoughts may differ, but we all are seeking permission to be seen. Some of us who need permission have been traumatized in childhood. Others have received subtle clues from their family that they are not worthy—through the look they give you, the lack of inclusion, the feelings of being invisible, all can be interpreted by the insecure person as messages. For example: "You are so fat, no one would want to be your friend. You are so ugly and boring, no one would want to be with you. Why do you bother to study when you are so stupid?" When our self-esteem gets smaller and smaller, our need to hide becomes bigger and bigger. Filled with doubt, we are paralyzed, unable to grow or risk moving forward.

Therapy Session—**Barter Love**

THERAPIST

Sometimes familiarity keeps us in our comfort zone. It doesn't feel good, but it fills our empty tank. "Do you love me? Am I lovable?" We repeat what happened when we were young. We continue playing that film in our minds because it is what we know.

MARGIE

An image just came up where I see little Margie performing for my father. I can see myself wanting to get attention from people that I love very much.

THERAPIST

Well, that's normal, but what we're looking for is the deficit.

MARGIE

The deficit?

THERAPIST

All right, let's do it this way. Let's tell a story of a child who didn't get love from her father and always wanted it. The child, not being supported, believed she wasn't good enough to get it. It's possible that her father gave her the messages of, "If you were a boy, I would love you." "If you were a better dancer, I'd love you." "If you were taller, I'd love you." So that's just human love blueprinting.

Now, let's change it again. What if you had the story that she marries a man, and he goes after someone else? She interprets his actions as, "If I had bigger boobs, or a bigger ass, or was smarter, or had more money, I would have been more lovable. I'm not lovable." So the message on the human plane is human attention from the desired ones: the lover, the father, the mother, or the child translates as therefore, I'm lovable. That's a barter love system.

MARGIE

So, the barter system keeps us in our comfort zone. We play those tapes saying the same thing over and over again, with different characters and different situations. If I do this for you, you will get that. It doesn't let us take any risks.

THERAPIST

That's what reincarnating keeps doing.

MARGIE

Over and over again, the same lessons over and over again, until
you learn them.

THERAPIST

Yes. What I'm saying to you is that because it's so deep, this
"barter love" is nonsense in your nervous system. It's that old.

MARGIE

So, it's more than expectations because it goes deeper than that.

THERAPIST

Yeah.

MARGIE

I remember when Michael was three years old. We were at the
San Diego Zoo. We passed a toy store and Michael, wanting a
new toy, immediately dropped on the sidewalk and refused to
move. He became hysterical, while I begged him to get up.
Nothing worked. I finally gave in and bought him a Batman toy.
He smiled and I could feel his love for me flooding back.

THERAPIST

There it is. The quintessential barter love system—all the mess
of parenting. I'm going to have you as a child, and later, I'm going
to want love and respect back.

　　We describe love as instrumental. So, let's you and I fall in
love and go live on the farm. Well, we need six or eight children.
There's a front pasture, a side pasture, and the cows and chickens.
We're going to need a lot of help. So, let's have a lot of children
so they can work the farm. That's called instrumental, right?

MARGIE

So, define instrumental.

THERAPIST

It's a service you provide.

MARGIE

Is it part of the barter system?

THERAPIST

It's part of human love, which doesn't sound very loving. Does it?

*A ship is always safe at shore,
but that is not what it's built for.*)

—Albert Einstein, theoretical physicist

Toni Garrn's Story—
From Food Poisoning to the Red Carpet

I was in Rwanda when I received a text from Margie. Besides being a model, I have a foundation for girls' education: we support secondary schooling for girls in different countries in Africa. Margie had been frantically texting me: "Stop whatever you are doing. I have a script that is perfect for you! Read it ASAP."

I read it and quickly realized that this was a very exciting role for me.

Whenever I could come to Los Angeles, I would jump into Margie's acting classes. I had a thirst for learning her philosophy but was still relatively new and uncomfortable in the acting world. Margie said they would start filming in about four weeks; I should send in a tape as soon as possible, and she would help me through it. Well, that would be an impossible undertaking and way out of my comfort zone in front of a crew of philanthropists in Africa!

Besides having to wake up at 6:00 a.m. every day to get to rural parts of Rwanda, after hours of driving, I had no time to tape anything, nor did I have anyone from that acting world with me, no clue how to find the right background or lighting, and no idea even how to upload a longer tape with a sporadic internet connection.

I was able to get on a Skype call with Margie and Fern Champion, the casting director, and she said, "If we prepare this now properly, and you do the right tape in two weeks, we will know if you got the part. Then you'll have to fly to Atlanta in a few days to start filming for six weeks."

So, I thought, *I'm going to have to give up this important trip to Rwanda as well as some already booked modeling jobs for the possibility of being hired?* On top of that, this role includes a South African accent (I'm German); I have zero time and no internet access to Skype for Margie to coach me—plus I had to go to a summit where I was meant to meet Barack Obama. That's right. *The* Barack Obama.

No way will this work.

I also questioned whether I could do such a huge part. Especially taking on what was a true and very tragic story.

One night, all of a sudden, my agent said she knew a filmmaker who could meet me in Spain, teach me the accent (in a day), and do the tapes with me.

Long story short, this messy tape led to Margie convincing the whole team and director that if I got the role, I'd have to be okay with arriving as the last person on set. I called Margie: "Is this crazy? I don't even know if I will book this part, and I'm giving everything up for it. I'm more comfortable staying in my own world."

Margie declared: "I believe in you. You're talented, and you can live the life of Reeva Steenkamp. She was a model. You are a model. You both look so much alike. It is a difficult part (she was murdered by Oscar Pistorius), but I'll get you through it."

If that wasn't challenging enough, the second I landed in Spain, I had a mix of what could have been food poisoning and malaria.

Being up all night throwing up, I was sent to a nearby hospital, and they gave me one of those life-changing IVs. I survived.

I finished the tapes. Margie looked at them first and told Fern that she thought there was some good stuff on them and to let the producer know that she would help me with the script. All this work was not for naught.

I booked the role! I had to move a few modeling jobs and had to stop in Los Angeles to work with Margie for the entire weekend before shooting in Atlanta. When I got the job, it hit me. *What am I doing here? How did I even get this job? Am I good enough?* I am thankful that I was able to work with Margie when I was in Atlanta.

It was all worth it, as I met the most incredible people on my team, from the English director, Norman Stone, to my love (and killer) on screen, Andreas, who actually was South African and helped me with the accent the whole six weeks of shooting and became my bestie on set.

I'm never going to forget this movie and definitely won't forget the process of getting it. This incredible adventure never would have happened if it weren't for Margie's faith in me. Also, I don't think I would have enjoyed the process of my first lead even half as much. And most of all, I was proud of myself for believing in myself and grateful for the help of others. It felt good to create such a fun project as a team.

And yes. I did get to meet Obama a day before heading to Los Angeles. My dream came true!

* Relationships! Relationships! Relationships! *

PAINTING ALL THE RED FLAGS BLUE

If we were willing to take risks, we'd choose healthier relationships. I'm a ten-year-relationship person. I just always "stay too long at the fair." I know, in my gut, that the relationship is dysfunctional, but I use the word "really" to keep the blinders on and stay in my comfort zone.

"She really is so different than she seems."

"If you really knew him, you would know he's really not like that."

"She is really a good person. She just gets anxious."

"He really does love me, he is just scared of intimacy."

"Really" statements keep us in denial. By living in denial, we are absolved of the responsibility of moving forward. If we have to look at the truth of how a relationship isn't working, we may have to leave and that would yank us out of our comfort zone.

It is not only the romantic relationships that we tend to stay in too long, but also friendships and professional ones. As we grow, our needs change. What worked for me when I was in my thirties does not necessarily work for me in this decade of life. I used to love to hang out with friends who liked to have a good time—go to parties, drink, smoke, get high. Those friends peeled off my life easily when my lifestyle changed. It was the needy friends, the ones who went through life as victims, that were hard to weed out. I felt too guilty to let them go, so I made excuses to avoid seeing them. Can you relate?

I have a friend whom I have known for fifty years. She has always taken up too much space for me. In earlier days, we fed off our mutual neuroses, which didn't help me grow or be happy or stay sane. By establishing boundaries, I limit my time with her as a way to honor and take care of myself.

Then, there are those of us who need to leave our comfort zone by asking for what we need or deserve.

Actors often don't like to make waves and, consequently, they lose their voice when working with an industry person. Reluctant to bother their agent or manager, they settle for not getting enough auditions, not getting feedback, or waiting endlessly to receive a phone call. They forget that the agent and the manager work for them and earn 10 percent. The actor is in charge. He or she who waits for permission is robbed of personal power. Many actors are also afraid to speak up in front of the casting director. It might be an important question, but the actor remains silent, and this kind of silence is toxic.

Trisha's Story—
"Hey, You Work for Me!"

I started out five years ago, represented by a small theatrical agency. I knew they could only take me so far in my career, but I was grateful to have representation. Two years ago, I realized they were not doing the job I needed them to do at that stage of my career. I was doing guest star spots, independent films, and various commercials, but they didn't have the clout to get me auditions as a series regular or for a studio film. I didn't complain. I guess I didn't want to sound ungrateful to them for starting me out. I was stuck.

Last year, I started working with Margie. From her teachings, I realized the reason I was not taking a meeting with my agents to discuss the issue was because I didn't want to get out of my comfort zone. Confronting someone, especially in business, was not my forte. Margie helped me look at why I stay stuck in that zone. I was afraid to be labeled a bad person. I was afraid I wouldn't find another agent. I was afraid to take a risk. Margie suggested that I take one step at a time. She told me to set up a meeting and lay out my concerns. Then give them three months to see if they could meet my realistic expectations. I also had to switch my viewpoint and remind myself that they worked for me. The meeting went well. I started going out on recurring and series regular auditions. Two months later, I booked a recurring role on a network series! I found my voice. I found my power."

If you risk nothing, then you risk everything.

—Geena Davis, actress

"I'M JUST BEING HONEST!"
ASSERTIVE VS. AGGRESSIVE

Being assertive is a different way of communicating than being aggressive. Assertive communication is the ability to express positive and negative ideas and feelings in an open, honest, and direct way. It recognizes our rights while still respecting the rights of others. It allows us to take responsibility for our actions and ourselves without judging or blaming other people.

Aggressive communication is a method of expressing needs and desires that does not take into account the welfare of others. Aggression brings out the worst in people. As a form of communication, it's often disguised as honesty. I can't tell you how many times I have heard, "I'm just being honest!"

The word "honest" gives people permission to attack and say hurtful things. "That outfit doesn't flatter you at all. You can't pull off that style. I'm just being honest."

Remember, truth without compassion is brutality.

There are those who feel comfortable in neutral, are afraid of being aggressive or receiving someone's aggressive reaction, so they choose passivity. They don't want to be a pincushion for someone's needles. Passivity applies to someone who accepts the actions or opinions of others without speaking up. The fear of making waves, which may incite an inappropriate reaction, can keep you in your comfort zone. However, by developing the skills of assertive communication, you will rise out of your protective space and claim your personal power.

AVOIDING RELATIONSHIPS

Some people never seek relationships. They are afraid of getting hurt, so they stay in their comfort zone of being alone. It is not that they prefer their own company, it's that they prefer to be safe. It's easy to fool ourselves, isn't it? We rationalize our isolation by thinking it makes us happier. By not allowing intimacy into our lives, we deny ourselves the chance to push the envelope. I have a friend who was my roommate in college. We were both single Jewish mothers who adopted our sons right after they were born, so we had a lot in common. Our sons went to the same school and became best friends. We would all do Hanukkah parties together where we made the best latkes. During all those years, my friend never went on a date. I would ask her if she missed intimacy with another person. Her answer was: "It's not worth it. There are too many negotiations, and emotional pain. I'm comfortable on my own." In my view, she sacrificed happiness for contentment. Was it really worth it?

> *And then the day came, when the*
> *risk to remain tight in a bud was more*
> *painful than the risk it took to blossom.*
>
> —Elizabeth Appell

∗ Living in the Unknown ∗

The fear of the unknown leaves us marooned in our comfort zone. It can spiral in all parts of our lives—relationships, work, vacations, promotions—any one of these opportunities can fall prey to our habit to stay closed up in our protective cave. Feeling safe is our only goal. But what would happen if we took the risk to embrace the unknown? That's way too scary for many of us. The irony is that the unknown is a place of growth and fulfillment. It's a place where we can own our power. It's a place where hopes and dreams become reality.

Michael John's Story— Take a Jump

'd been in the same job for eighteen years. It had started out as the ideal job—creative and forward-thinking, with opportunities to be daring and take risks. Over the years, with new leadership, things changed. The job became restrictive, and my creativity felt stunted. It didn't seem to matter that I was not challenging myself every day. I was safe, but not happy, and I stayed because I knew what I had and was too afraid to step in the unknown.

It all changed when I went on a break in New York with my partner. I'd flown out late on a Wednesday night after a particularly difficult week where I'd allowed myself to become dejected and disheartened. I was looking forward to being in New York but could not stop thinking about the work I'd have to deal with when I got back to London.

I FaceTimed Margie. She had been a close friend for a number of years. We had first met through my job, where she did a powerful workshop. I visited her several times a year. With her being Los Angeles-based, it was strange to be in the United States and not see her. She knew something was wrong and chatted with me openly, asking me questions that made me think wider than my work situation. I'd known Margie's approach for years but, to my regret, only at this low point did I start applying it to my life. Why stay where I was unhappy? Aren't you worth more than that? Take a jump, get out of your comfort zone, and see what opportunities open up.

Men of my generation had always been taught to avoid vulnerability. Strength was about keeping your head down, staying stoic, and fighting on. Margie helped refocus and redefine my priorities. I felt myself standing on a threshold.

I made a decision that day to leave my job. I had a great time in New York once I'd made that decision. And the minute I handed in my notice, new opportunities started to roll in. I embraced the unknown, made myself vulnerable, took a risk, lost control, and found a stronger version of myself.

The only thing that is stopping you from where you are to where you want to go is your comfort zone.

—Dhaval Gaudier

Ivana Baquero's Story— My Life Changed Overnight

My life changed overnight when, at eleven years old, director Guillermo del Toro chose me as the lead in *Pan's Labyrinth*.

I immediately had to step out of my comfort zone: from the auditioning process where I was told to prepare some material and then given completely new sides upon arrival, to shooting away from home and school. And then, stepping further out of my comfort zone, I discovered a whole new world during the promotion of the movie: from press conferences and junkets around the world, to film festivals, parties, and awards ceremonies.

As time went by, just when I thought I found my footing, I once again had to step out of my comfort zone. I had to transition from a child actor to an adult actor.

Imagine building a successful career from scratch and then having to start all over again, because you have, essentially, become a different person both physically and emotionally. That's what the transition felt like, and often it still feels like that.

I had to prove myself again, and show casting directors, producers, and the industry that I was able to carry my talent into this adult version of myself.

The only way to move forward was to take another risk by dividing my time between Spain and Los Angeles. And that, as exciting as it was, was a scary leap of faith. In that journey to discover myself as an adult actor, I was met with a very interesting dichotomy: finding myself as an adult, period. I was presented with new experiences, challenges, and a lot of life-altering opportunities. I moved to New Zealand to shoot a show for a couple years, I fell in love, then I went back to Spain for another job that had me travelling back and forth for a couple more years. Suddenly there I was, pushing through fears and discovering a brand new horizon of opportunities that allowed me to grow profoundly both professionally and personally.

PROCRASTINATION— SUCCESS/FAILURE SYNDROME

Many people feel more comfortable putting off decisions or actions. Procrastination allows us to not make choices, which is a way of staying put in a comfort zone.

As a college student in upstate New York, I suffered from an overwhelming success/failure syndrome. I was afraid to study because if I didn't get an A or a B, I would accuse myself of not being smart enough. So, I put off studying, or would study the night before an exam. If I received a C in the class, it meant I wasn't stupid because I got that grade with no studying. I wasn't taking responsibility for the outcome. Often, procrastinators are labeled lazy. The reality is that it's a bad habit developed from a fear of failure. Even success is daunting. The fear of not staying in the "win" can be brutal. Fear of the unknown is an agent of procrastination.

MARGISM:
PULL THE PLUG ON PROCRASTINATION

Steps to pull the plug on procrastination:

1. Admit you have a problem and where it occurs.
2. Take small steps, beginning with one specific area where you put off your tasks.
3. Validate each time you meet your challenge. Claim your victory, large and small.
4. Forgive yourself when you don't meet your challenge.
5. Consider it a bad habit, not a character default.

You don't have to be great to start,

but you do have to start to be great.

— Zig Ziglar, author and motivational speaker

James Morgan's Story—
On with the Show!

My goal was to create my own one-man show with music. It excited me, but it also terrified me. I had never written anything before, and I can't write music.

Friends and colleagues would regularly ask me: "How is your show coming along? When can we come and see it?" I would always make some excuse that it was on pause because of other work commitments, costs, and lack of time. The truth: I was terrified. What if an audience does not like my stories? What if they don't like my song choices? What if I don't get an audience? *What if, what if, what if!!!*

This fear became crippling. I became static. There was only one thing worse than creating this show and that was *not* creating this show.

So, I found a collaborator to work on my script with me, and I found a venue to premiere my show. Now all I had to do was to create a show. So, what comes first, the stories or the songs? If I thought saying "yes" was a step out of my comfort zone, I was in for an even bigger surprise when it came to creating the work.

My singing voice has often been compared to that of George Michael, a compliment I wholeheartedly embrace.

I thought it would be interesting to take a collection of George's music, songs that I had listened to from childhood to adulthood, and weave them around my own story, like a soundtrack to my life. I have loved George's music from a very young age. I love the unforgettable melodies and his rich, mellifluous voice. But it was more than that. I had no idea, at the time, but there was angst in his music, awkwardness when he spoke about himself, and a vulnerability in him that I could totally relate to. Growing up as a sensitive boy in a tough, working-class, Welsh village, I would lose myself in songs and movies. I only had to hear an old George song, and I was transported back to a time where I was maybe lovesick or homesick or falling in love. That was my one-man show!

And so I started to piece together my own stories of growing up a sensitive beta male in an alpha male world: stories of my blissfully happy home life against my tormented, bullied, school life, my sexuality, and nearly losing the love of my life for fear of coming out.

I wove these personal stories in with songs by George that had kept me company over the years. My show was finally written, music arranged, band and venue booked. Now I had to make the biggest step out of my comfort zone and share these personal stories and feelings with a room full of strangers. Yet again, the inner critic found its voice. *What if they get bored? Do you really have anything to say? What if they just want songs and you are talking too much?*

I let my inner critic have his say then I asked him to leave. Removing myself from my comfort zone, I went on with the show.

Studio Focus: **Conversations from the Classroom**
LIVING IN YOUR COMFORT ZONE DURING COVID-19

INT. CLASSROOM—DAY

MARGIE

Today, I want to talk about your comfort zone. What is your go-to, and how do you get out of it?

JACK

I broke out of my comfort zone when I started performing live on my piano on social media every Sunday night. It has been once a week for three months, and I still get nervous. But I am risking it.

MARGIE

I can't wait to take piano lessons from you! So, class, what challenges have caused you to get out of your box? Feeling safe does not allow you to step out of your comfort zone.

SALLY

My normal way is to throw myself into something but, because of the COVID pandemic restrictions, I have been sitting with myself instead of going somewhere. At first, I was horrified that I didn't have a gig for a year, but now it's allowing me to get out of the comfort zone of running.

TAYLOR

In the past, I had such crippling anxiety I couldn't get out of bed. I was nervous about being isolated, but my meditation practice has leveled out my anxiety. I started Deepak Chopra's "21-Day Abundance Meditation Course" offered online.

JACKSON

Being stuck in my comfort zone is to stay in my apartment and not do anything. I'm new to Los Angeles, so driving really scares me. I took a job delivering food. I go to the grocery store, which is totally out of my comfort zone, seeing I have never food-shopped! Hey, cut me some slack. I'm only eighteen! It's helping me to grow up, and it feels really good when I drop the groceries off at the door. I feel like I am doing something meaningful, even though I have anxiety about it.

MARGIE

When you peak out of that safe place, all that fear goes away and the joy of helping others will guide you.

ANTHONY

I am playing guitar, and I started posting videos so I can take accountability and get feedback and allow my artistic juices to flow.

MARGIE

Mel, how has the coronavirus affected you? What are the challenges?

MEL

I try to do self-care. I sleep a lot. I start the morning with a gratitude meditation, and I am addicted to a couple of video games on the phone.

AMY

I am up and down. It is hard to get out of my comfort zone, which is stuffing my feelings down and not looking at them. So, I write morning pages of stream of consciousness. I am writing a show about what is going on in the world. I dive in and it grounds me.

MARGIE

Recently, I realized that I am triggered by those closest to me. I close off and shut down in order to protect myself instead of being true to who I am. When you examine your comfort zone, it uncovers how you get in the way of being seen by others. So, where have you taken risks? Maddie?

MADDIE

I used to be bad with conflict. During this confinement, I realize I don't need the external validation anymore. I started using my voice. I learned to say no, understanding that my needs come first.

MARGIE

So proud of you! It is an erroneous belief that your life will be happy if you can get outside validation. It feels good when you speak up. Not feeling heard gets in your way of having healthy relationships. Your self-esteem is more intact by loving yourself.

KIMBERLEY

I am not a people pleaser, but I am at my best when I am helping people. I like to put my ego aside to help them be the best they can be. This time has made me wonderfully selfish.

MARGIE

Kimberley, there is power in saying no. Many of us come from wanting to be seen. I am afraid of being invisible so I struggle with boundaries and say yes too often. How about you, Sarah?

SARAH

I'm not doing well today.

MARGIE

How can you help yourself to get out of being stuck?

SARAH

I guess finding a way to jump out, which I haven't found yet.

MARGIE

First, you have to fill up your own tank. I know Kimberley mentioned that during this time she was being selfish, but the word needs to be changed to "self-full." This is not a selfish act; it is a self-full act. Then we will have room to help others.

STEVE

I have a lot of free time, and I don't know what to do with it. When I'm busy, I don't have a moment to think, but when I'm not, I am afraid of wasting my life.

MARGIE

I run around constantly doing something. It's more comfortable for me to always stay active. But, if you can sit with the discomfort, even though it's challenging, you can get to know yourself so much better.

BETSY

Keeping myself in my office and working creatively is safe but getting out there seeking relationships is frightening. Once I am in the middle of it, I'm fine. It's getting started, that's the problem.

MARGIE

Most of us have trouble getting started. When we are in it, we are fine. When I'm writing, it's great. Actually sitting down to start writing is the big challenge.

PETER

All I ever seem to do is beat myself up.

MARGIE

Ironically, beating yourself up is comfortable for you. It is something you are used to, even though it doesn't feel good. It is a bad habit.

CARY

My comfort zone is my day job. It's not very difficult. I need to let go of the excuse that I have worked all day and be willing to go home and write and do something creative for myself.

MARGIE

Your awareness is that first step. Now you can take action.

ANTHONY

I watch a lot of television. And I wish I could do what they are doing, but I don't do anything to get myself there.

MARGIE

So, it is comfortable to be in your world of fantasy, and uncomfortable to take action on it.

IRINA

I preplan like hell to avoid the unknown. It's too scary to me.

MARGIE

It's a fear for all of us. I have this false belief that knowing where I am going in life will be good for me. It's actually the opposite. Being safe is not a goal. It controls us. Being open to whatever will happen fills our life with joy and makes everything an adventure.

The hardest thing to do is leaving your comfort zone. But you have to let go of the life you're familiar with and take the risk to live the life you dream about.

—T. Arigo

TRUST

Trust in the power of trust. A child who comes from an abusive environment lives a life that is steeped in fear, and this paves the way to lack of trust. Even those of us who were loved as children face similar challenges. Along with not trusting others, we can fall prey to not trusting ourselves, and this is the core problem. Above all else, the person you need to trust the most is yourself. Trust that you're enough. Trust that you have the power to make the right choices to fulfill your life. Trust in your talent and skills. Trust in your willingness to learn, grow, and evolve. Trust in your gut instincts. When you trust yourself, you can take risks and get out of your comfort zone. Trust yourself, and you will be the lead in your own life.

THREE STEPS OUT
OF YOUR COMFORT ZONE

1. Acknowledge

The first step is to acknowledge that your comfort zone is not serving you. Acknowledgment is a victory in itself. Now imagine a door that you can open to a life bursting with possibilities. Be willing to acknowledge that there is a way out and a better life waiting for you. It will motivate you to action.

2. Take Action

Now that you've acknowledged the problem, you can take action and confidently stride through the door. When you are stuck in neutral, or even terrified of neutral and of taking up too much space, apply the S-T-O-P method: Stop. Take a breath. Observe. Proceed. If you still feel fear about proceeding, choose to say, "Fuck it." "Fuck it" is a declaration of freedom. It announces to the world that nothing can hold you back, not even your fear. Although fear can be crippling at times, it can also be a powerful catalyst for positive change. We are all fearful.

There is nothing wrong with it. Recast your fear. It can become a motivating factor. Use it to launch into a higher orbit of creativity.

3. Accept

This is huge and challenging for many of us.

When I am in my comfort zone, I am not accepting that it is okay to be fearful and to live in reality. What happened to me when I was young is something I can't change. I can accept it and move forward. No one gets away in life without having struggles and dark times. We must accept them and know they are part of life's journey. Accept your limitations. Accept that you have fear. Accept all imperfections and embrace them. Accept being a human. If we each could live in acceptance, we would all be happier.

MARGISM

Courage isn't the absence of fear; it's not giving in to fear.

Tom Brady,
the Spirit of Determination

As a lifelong New England Patriots fan, I am a true admirer of quarterback Tom Brady, a seven-time Super Bowl champion. He can not only connect with his brilliant touchdown passes on the football field, he connects with millions of people around the world as a role model of determination.

Tom generously acknowledges all the people in his life: family, coaches, teammates, and other mentors who supported his goals and success. He appreciates those who told him he should never put limits on his abilities, and those who coached him to live up to his talents and never give up.

Tom has spent his share of time on the bench—not being chosen and sometimes overlooked. He counts himself lucky for those hardships, saying that they gave him both the heart and the will to keep going, the greatest edge of all.

Tom knew that he wasn't alone in his fear of failure, that everyone goes through it. The magic is in trying again and not giving up. As he advises others, one day you'll look back and be grateful for every struggle. Don't give up. Heart and will always find a way.

> The truth is that our finest moments
> are most likely to occur when we are
> feeling deeply uncomfortable,
> unhappy, or unfulfilled. For it is only in
> such moments, propelled by our
> discomfort, that we are likely to step
> out of our ruts and start searching for
> different ways or truer answers.

—M. Scott Peck,
author of *The Road Less Traveled*

POWER CHALLENGE

- What is your comfort zone? Describe it. What bad habits keep you stuck in neutral?
- When you reflect on your life, how do you think your comfort zone habits developed? Be honest, while using self-kindness.

- Ask yourself, "Do I want to be happy, or do I want to be comfortable?" Write down your response and then sit with it.
- Are you waiting for permission from others to go further in your life? If you used the magic words, "Fuck it," in your life today, how would they help you move forward?
- Is there a concern that you might be too aggressive or too passive? Find three incidents where you can change a conversation from aggressive or passive to assertive.
- Write about three past experiences where you procrastinated. Then write down three ways you can change that behavior. Remind yourself it's okay to be imperfect. We each have three projects or dreams being held up by our own procrastination. What are yours? List them, accept your imperfections, and then write down beginning actions to get out of that comfort zone.
- Write down three examples of either taking up too much space or not enough. What actions would change that in an empowering way, taking you out of your comfort zone?

3

Am I a Drama Queen in Disguise? Rescuer, Victim, Persecutor

You've heard of the Bermuda Triangle, right? Ships, aircrafts, and a number of human beings have mysteriously disappeared within that geographic triangle. But, there's another triangle that can swallow up the adult you. This one is fascinating because it has three distinct points: Rescuer, Victim, and Persecutor. These are the roles we play while interacting with others. It's been defined as the Karpman Drama Triangle, the connection between personal responsibility and power in conflicts.

Most of us don't realize that we are participating in this unhealthy communication as we shift between one of the three roles. Within one conversation, we can go from Rescuer to Victim to Persecutor, doomed to repeat the same scenario until we find our way out of the triangle and into a more elevated state of consciousness called the Adult.

Do you walk around as a Victim, a Rescuer, or a Persecutor? It is in these three states of mind where the Drama Queen builds her throne. It's how she rules her life and everyone in it. What she doesn't realize is that the triangle actually rules *her*! And guess what, guys? You can be a drama queen too!

* Drama Queen *

Here's one scenario in a Drama Queen's day: Someone says to you, "That long shirt looks good on you."

Ding, Ding, Ding!

You may go into Victim mode, feeling criticized. Victim springs to the defense. "Do you think I'm fat? Is that what you're saying?"

That small exchange caused your self-esteem to shrink, and you lost personal power. You might have misinterpreted what the person's intentions were, but because you were looking through the Victim lens, that's where the conversation went.

Or the "long shirt" conversation could go a different and equally unhelpful direction.

"Are you telling me I'm fat? Well, you're not looking that good either. You need to lose some weight too!" That snapping remark hurls you to another point on the triangle, the Persecutor. There's nothing Adult about that response.

Now, let's imagine a third scenario. You are the one who overhears this contentious conversation between two friends regarding being overweight. You leap in to save the day. "Hey, I know a great place for a low-calorie lunch." You are reacting from the third part of the triangle point—the Rescuer. It may seem like a reasonable place to be, but is it really? After you suggest a low-carb restaurant, your two friends may say in unison, "Oh, so you *do* think we're fat? Screw you!" In that moment, you drop into Victim mode. Can you see what is happening?

MARGISM

There are two different worlds, the light world and the dark world.
The question is: Which one wins?
Answer: The one you feed, baby. The one you feed.

Studio Focus: **Conversations from the Classroom**
MARRIED LIFE, HOME OF THE TRIANGLE

INT. CLASSROOM–DAY

SALLY

I am predominantly a Rescuer. Whenever there's a problem, I
have to be the solution finder! I don't know if part of that is a
pride thing where I'm smarter than everyone else, and I'm
gonna have all the answers or—I think part of rescuing is also
that the light is not on you and your insecurities or problems.
Right? But you're shining them on other people. I've gotten
pretty good at it. I go through life without any drama, aside from
when I'm with my husband.

The class chuckles.

He makes one little remark. I get defensive immediately. I
become the Persecutor with him straight away, and then I'm
crying like a total Victim.

MARGIE

What you're saying, Sally, is—this is what's so fascinating—
especially if you want to play a character that's similar, you go to
Persecutor and then become a Victim.

SALLY

Yeah, all these things are ways I manipulate other people, even
if I don't understand it in the moment. Maybe I'm too proud, or

I've made a mistake, or he's got a point about something. I'll be too proud to say so.

MARGIE

You want to be in control, and you're afraid of vulnerability. In a marriage, it is very common to get stuck in this triangle. The triangle is three 60-degree angles that corner you in a prison of dysfunction. You have to break out.

> *It is true . . . that the real tragedy*
> *in our time is that any of us can be,*
> *interchangeably, victim or torturer.*

—Jean-Paul Sartre, author and French philosopher

* Victim—In the Spotlight *

"Poor me. No one understands me. They don't love me. My family is the cause of my misery. I can't believe he gave that job to her, not to me."

Victims may want to be rescued, but they don't want to be reminded of their inadequacies. Not taking responsibility for their actions is the hallmark of Victim behavior. Another defining characteristic is oversensitivity and clinging to their glass-half-empty perspective of life.

For me, the glass is always overflowing. I never saw myself as a Victim and didn't accept Victim behavior from others who chose to live in past traumas and act small. I, on the other hand, fill the room with my presence, so I was surprised to know the Victim exists inside me. The Victim in my own triangle arises when I think people are judging me, especially those I care about most, like my son. Years of therapy to understand my behavior helped me see it and take responsibility for being the lead in my life.

Oversensitivity is the silent
cause of all suffering.

—Anonymous

HIT ME WITH A GOLF CLUB

I am an old tennis player who also tries to play golf. I don't know much about the proper etiquette, or the technical part of the game, or even how to swing really, but my athletic ability allows the ball to go forward. One day, while putting on the fourth hole, I walked through the middle of the putting ground, where the balls were surrounding the hole.

My golf partner reprimanded me. "Don't walk in the middle. It is improper."

Well, you would have thought someone hit me with the golf club. My shoulders dropped, and I sank into Victim mode. My thoughts were like a virus in my brain—they had taken over. *How could she say that to me in the middle of the game? How dare she talk to me like that! She's supposed to be my friend!* I tried changing my focus by looking at the sky, but my thoughts were like a faucet of gushing water, and I couldn't close the valve.

Lucky for me, it was therapy day, and I told my therapist about my experience. My golf partner had cited me with a verbal ticket for breaking etiquette on the golf course. First, I had to label it for what it was, shame. It's just shame, yet it's my most dreaded emotion. Still, I could forgive it. I could let it go. This neutralizes the big-deal-ness of it. Then, to shift out of the negative experience, I replaced it with one of love. I immediately saw my mother's ocean-blue eyes smiling at me with adoration and pride. My Victim mode melted away.

Bella's Story—
My Dysfunctional Family

I was nine years old when I witnessed an act of violence between my parents. It was a terrible fight, and it will be etched in my memory forever. My mom left my dad, moving my brother and me to New York. She told us stories of how terrible he was and that he never wanted to see us. We grew up believing those stories were true. My mom was the victim, and I was determined to rescue her. I became a true people pleaser. Whatever my mom and brother needed, I provided in a flash. When I got married, they were both jealous of my husband. He was never allowed to come to any family functions. I accepted this because I didn't want to make waves, but then I switched into a Victim role. *My family doesn't love me. After all I have sacrificed for my mother and brother, this is how they treat me? They are the cause of all the pain in my life.*

While this part of my family was falling apart, I decided to call my dad.

I hadn't spoken to him since my mom poisoned me with her hatred for him. We spoke a few times, and then he came to New York to visit me. He turned out to be a great guy. I invited my mom and brother to see him. It had been thirty years, but they wanted to stay in their Victim roles. I heard various responses from them, such as: "You don't love us enough. If you did love us, you wouldn't have any relationship with him. You are a traitor."

It was then that I realized how ugly it is to be a Victim. For the first time, I responded as an Adult.

I told them: "I love you both but if you want to be in my life, you need to treat my husband with respect. It is up to you to let go of the past with Dad. If you choose not to, then I will accept it."

With that one phone call, all the weight on my chest disappeared, and I understood what it meant to be free of the expectations and dramatizations I had created in my life. Freedom felt so good!

Therapy Session—
"But It Feels So Good When I Complain!"

MARGIE

Complaining has been my unconscious go-to in the Victim role. It's just so easy! I'm in an automatic state. As soon as I wake up, unattractive groans are released with a "kvetching" (Jewish for *complaining*) behavior. Thank God for therapy!

THERAPIST

When you were carrying your dog, Georgie, back home, it sounded like you were complaining in your head. So, what are you doing by complaining?

MARGIE

I was letting off steam, but it wasn't useful. So, what could I have done differently?

THERAPIST

The problem is that the complaining may have been the fire under the pot, making the steam. So, if you think complaining or venting is useful, then you're in trouble. Letting off steam is going for a swim and looking at the beautiful backyard.

MARGIE

Right.

THERAPIST

What do you want from it? Let's set the stage. You walk on stage right, and the other person is stage left, and then you complain. And then what do you want that character to do in response that is ideally rewarding?

MARGIE

"Oh, Margie, that must be so horrible for you not to sleep all night and to be in so much pain. Can I help you out? What can I do for you?" That's what I want.

THERAPIST

Is there anything else you want?

MARGIE

A hug.

THERAPIST

All right. So, be direct, not indirect. Walk onto the stage with that noise in your body and weight on your shoulders and say to her, "Can I have a hug? Thank you so much."

When did you start complaining? You didn't sleep well, and the body has got a lot of noise in it, and then your puppy dog suddenly doesn't want to walk.

MARGIE

It feels so good when I'm complaining.

THERAPIST

Which is partly why it gets coded as a habit, because of the feel-good part.

MARGIE

It keeps me talking, but it doesn't help me be an adult.

THERAPIST

Make an assessment. Oh, this dog's just not up for it. I guess we're going home. Let me pick him up. And look at the neighbor's yard and how they cut the grass, it's gorgeous.

MARGIE

So, it dilutes the emotional reaction.

THERAPIST

What's the plan? What would be good for me? Make choices. Should I have some chocolate pie? Should I lie outside, or should I find a firing squad? Should I take a swim? Should I take a nap?

MARGIE

I can just rub my neck and not tell everybody that I'm in agony. Complaining, "Oh, my neck is killing me. I slept wrong all night. Oh my God, my back is killing me."

THERAPIST

I'm going to barf some toxic fumes out at you, and then I want you to hug me. It's unbecoming.

MARGIE

Wow. Bad habits. Rather than dramatizing it, go back to the Adult. What can I do to take care of myself? I think I'll take a swim.

THERAPIST

Yeah. Do it, and then you'll reevaluate. When you are in your complaining mode, how old are you, really?

MARGIE

About six or seven.

THERAPIST

Uh-huh.

MARGIE

And I want my attention. I end up having a PhD in being a Victim. I have to turn that degree in!

THERAPIST

It's so commonplace. We live in a culture of complaints. It keeps us in the drama.

My moms always told me,

"How long you gonna play the victim?"

I can say I'm mad and I hate everything, but

nothing really changes until I change myself.

—Kendrick Lamar, rap artist

* Rescuer—The Fixer *

"I am a people pleaser" is the Rescuer's mantra. The Rescuer's job is to keep everyone happy as if it was within his or her power to do so. The Rescuer feels responsible for handling everything. "I am smart, unselfish, and really good at helping others."

At the time, it feels like the Rescuer is doing it all with no strings attached, but that is rarely the case.

"I am going to help him feel better since he had such a difficult day at work. I will take all the responsibilities of our child and the house, even though I worked all day as well."

Then, when our partner doesn't fulfill our smallest expectations, you can quickly become the martyred Rescuer. "I can't believe how little you appreciate me. After all I have done to save you!"

STAY IN MY OWN LANE

Do you believe you have the answer to fixing people's feelings and rescuing them from themselves? It's an unhealthy antenna. Within your core belief is the thought that you're Moses and have the superpower to make everyone happy. Your self-esteem is attached to wanting to help others who probably didn't want it. When someone is standing on the edge of a cliff, it's hard to watch without interfering.

In my own Rescuer mode, I would have anxiety thinking that something terrible would happen to my friends and family if I didn't step in and point out their problems. Can't they see I am doing this because I love them? I'm the good guy here!

I love my son, and all I want is for him to have the best life possible. But do I trust that he can do this on his own? Emphatically—*no*. I have been a helicopter parent from the day Michael was born. I enabled him by not staying in my own lane. It was only later in his life that I finally understood my job as a parent—to let him fall as far as he needs to until he grows his own wings. I can help him become an adult if I am an adult myself. I can give him the dignity of knowing he can take care of himself. I can take my own temperature, not his.

I've learned to "zip it" and not think I have the answers to someone else's life. I keep my "constructive criticism" to myself. I have to let go of this bad habit and give him the opportunity to find his path. It sounds easy, but my God, is it difficult! It's easy to be a Rescuer but to detach with love is the bigger challenge. I've made steps by replacing judgment with curiosity.

When we realize we are powerless over their behavior and only responsible for our own happiness, we can give up being a Drama Queen.

Cheryl's Story— I Had to Take the Bus

My daughter had a drug problem, which was exacerbated by my need to be the fixer. I thought I had the answers to help her. I needed to completely cut those strings and let her be on her own. We didn't see her. We didn't speak to her. She was cut off completely for a year—the hardest thing I have ever done. Friends of mine would say: "How could you do it? What if she dies? You don't even know where she is."

At some point during this time, she called me, and during the conversation, I heard her say, "Yeah, I'll have the chicken with Swiss cheese."

I said, "Where are you?"

And she said, "Well, I'm at the Beverly Hills Country Club order-ing a sandwich." She thought that was our place, and she could just go there and get a sandwich on our account even though we had completely cut her off.

I said, "Here's what I need you to do. I need you to get up and leave right now."

She hung up on me and left, and that was it. That was how I had to parent her to get her well.

I always tried to rescue her, to fix it. I'm all about the solution, and the solution was always rescuing everyone.

My daughter was very entitled—we would get her a cell phone, she would lose a cell phone, and then "Mommy will get you another cellphone," until she lost that one too. Then, when she was using drugs, we gave her a couple of chances, and then we just said: "That's it. You're on your own."

I realized that I had to have the guts to walk away. That's the hard part, because it's really about us as parents. We get this glow from fixing our children. Our hearts beat fast. We're going to solve it.

What's the definition of crazy? Doing the same thing over and over again and expecting different results. Clearly, I saw the results. I saw the fruits of my labor, and it was dark. I mean, my daughter crashed a car going in the opposite direction on the freeway, going a hundred miles an hour, totaling the car. So, when, by the grace of God, she lived through it, I knew that I had to change.

When my daughter got well, and she did, and got sober, she was an amazing, beautiful, successful woman who helped other families' kids get sober. They would ask her, "What was the single biggest thing that you did that helped you get sober?" And she said, "My parents helped me. I had to take the bus." She went from being a young woman in a BMW, private golf club, and elite private schools to living on the streets.

I was a Rescuer all my life because I never felt my parents knew what they were doing. By the time I was five years old, I was already solving the problems for the family. All my friendships were like that. "I will solve this for you. I will find you the right place to live. And don't worry, Cheryl's here and let me decorate your place. *And let me, let me, let me, let me, let me.*" That was how I got my self-worth, by fixing everyone. When I stopped doing it, I went through a period of *Who am I? What am I?*

If I define myself through rescuing other people, then who am I when I stop rescuing them? I had to figure out what my void was and then fill it with something healthy. I realize all relationships require you to let go.

To stay in a marriage, to be in a successful marriage, you have to let go. And my mind has been programmed, since I'm still a little kid, to go from my brain to my mouth, and then it all comes straight out. "Put that there. Don't put the top on like that. Are those socks clean?" I mean, whatever it was, I had the thought, and it would come out of my mouth. But I don't do that anymore.

I have learned to just let things be, because I want to have a successful relationship. I was married for fifteen years, divorced for five, then remarried the same guy for eight. And we have a great, successful, fun, happy, funny relationship.

We have a mutual appreciation and trust so that we don't need to continually "fix" or "rescue," which is part of staying in your own lane. You're always going to see the stuff that bugs you. That's how we're wired. But the right behavior is to not respond. Reacting to it is what changes. I love the saying, "Does it need to be said? Does it need to be said by me? Does it need to be said right now?"

*Keep your attention focused entirely
on what is truly your own concern, and
be clear that what belongs to others
is their business and none of yours.*

—Epictetus, stoic philosopher

Studio Focus: Conversations from the Classroom
OXYGEN MASK

INT. CLASSROOM–DAY

PETER
I always fall back on the Rescuer. It shorts me of what I need to do for myself because I tend to be very selfless by being the Rescuer. I don't think or take care of myself. I've learned that sometimes I have to be a little selfish—

MARGIE
I call it *self-full.*

PETER
Yes! Exactly.

MARGIE

When you're a Rescuer, you don't want to deal with your stuff, because you don't think you're a good person if you take care of yourself first.

PETER
Yeah, and I usually say that I take care of others better than I take care of myself.

MARGIE
You've heard, "When you are on a plane, put your oxygen mask on first, then take care of somebody else." Do you end up

becoming a Persecutor or a Victim if it doesn't work out for you?

PETER

I don't become a Persecutor 'cause I feel like it doesn't accomplish anything. It's a battle that's not worth fighting unless you go about it sensibly.

MARGIE

So, you really do stay a lot in the rescue place? You don't have an angry part of you that attacks someone when the Rescuer doesn't work?

PETER

I keep it in.

MARGIE

When you are a Rescuer, it is hard to communicate. There is a fear that you will lose someone if you don't put her needs over yours. You also get to be the special one everyone can count on. It's very addictive. Peter you can be kind without rescuing. Focus on the relationship with yourself. You deserve it.

TAKE THE MONEY, I'LL FEEL BETTER

I always thought I was a good person. When I first moved to Santa Monica from Long Island, years ago, I would get out of my car at any stop sign to help an old woman cross the street, whether she needed it or not. I just couldn't stay in my own lane. When I walked down the famous 3rd Street Promenade, I was horrified by how many homeless women would be crouched in a corner with a child. I limited myself to giving one dollar to each of ten people. With every step, I saw old, torn sleeping bags pocketing a desperate woman or man who seemingly lived without hope.

There was a mentally ill homeless woman who appeared to be older than seventy. Many psychiatric hospitals had lost their funding and discharged their patients, leaving them to provide for themselves on the streets. Whenever I passed this woman, she would be lost in a conversation with herself. I handed her a twenty-dollar bill one day as I pushed my son in his stroller. As I left, I heard her cry out to me: "Stop. Take back your money. I don't take money from mothers with little children."

I never saw her after that day. She seemed to have disappeared. I felt guilty that I might have caused her to leave. She had her pride, had not asked to be rescued, and in all honesty, the driving force in giving her money was to make myself feel better.

THE TUGBOAT
VERSUS THE LIGHTHOUSE

The tugboat maneuvers other vessels by pushing and pulling them. It can push a big barge in foul weather. It is dirty and grimy, but it does its job.

A lighthouse guides vessels using a rotating, flashing light at the top. The lighthouse performs the same function as a tugboat, but it stays out of the water. It guides ships without getting messy and damaged.

Do we humans have to drag ourselves through the mud, or can we stand tall and graceful and guide others by being a lighthouse?

Love is letting others voluntarily evolve.

—Shana Olmstead, intuitive consultant

* Persecutor—The Bully *

When the Rescuer doesn't get what she wants, and the Victim can't be heard, out comes the Persecutor. The Persecutor's mandate is to always be right and win, no matter what. We give ourselves carte blanche to preach, blame, lecture, interrogate, and attack. The Persecutor strikes out to feel better—crying, "It's all your fault," the Persecutor wins the battle but loses the war.

Studio Focus: Conversations from the Classroom
BLAME GAME, THE SILENT TREATMENT

INT. CLASSROOM—DAY

MARGIE
We think that the Persecutor yells to get a point across, but the deadliest weapon is the silent treatment.

BARBARA
I do that with my husband.

CARY
I do it with my sister.

MARGIE
The silent treatment is passive-aggressive. It can also be a form of avoidance.

BETO
I don't talk to people for a long time. You screw me up, and you're cut off.

MARGIE
Why do you think you do that?

BETO
Because ... it's just in my astrology? I'm a Libra Sun with a Sagittarius moon.

MARGIE

Thank you for being so clever. The statement, "You screw me up, and you're cut off," is the Persecutor. But it's the Victim as well.

BETO

I don't really feel like a victim.

MARGIE

There are different ways to experience being the Victim. The Victim is not always saying, "Oh, I feel so sorry for myself." The Victim can also cause us to stop talking and shut down because we're scared. So, underneath the Persecutor can be the Victim as well.

BETO

Yeah, I never thought of it that way.

> *There really is no difference*
> *between the bully and the victim.*
>
> —Lady Gaga

RETALIATION— THEY HAD IT COMING

Do you feel better when you retaliate? Do you get a sense of joy when you get back at someone who hurt your feelings? If you do, you are not alone. I always think I'm a good person until I slip into that place of false power. It feels good when I win but at what price?

Imagine picking up hot coals with your bare hands to throw in retaliation at the person who hurt you or made you angry. For a brief moment, it feels good to release your rage on them until you look at your hands, which are severely burned.

How do you keep from burning your hand? What is the small victory to step out of the triangle and take the high road?

MARGISM: LOSE THE ATTITUDE

1. Ask an adult question without an attitude.
2. Take that calming breath, turn, and walk away.
3. Tease yourself with a made-up song. As you turn away from the person who hurts you, try singing: "I'm so immature. I am getting hijacked by my immaturity."

Lee Donoghue's Story— Striking Back

Lee was an adorable, sweet man who always wanted to help me get ready for my next class. He was helpful to everyone and willing to share parts of himself as long as they were more on the superficial side. When his vulnerability was exposed, he got defensive and attacked.

Lee came to me with a successful career in New Zealand and soon, like most actors who come from a small pond to this vast ocean called Los Angeles, his bubble was burst by the amount of competition. Lee kept his vulnerability hidden under a cocky attitude. He never wanted to share anything that would expose his fear of not achieving his specific goals as an actor.

In my ongoing classes, each week, I would either give him a cold read where he only had a short time to create a scene, or a warm read where he could have a few days. I remember giving the class a comedy slice of life.

His reaction was: "I don't do comedy. I am a dramatic actor."

My reaction was: "Really? I didn't know that creating a life was limited to a specific genre. Creation is creation." *Drama/Comedy*

He protested in his Persecutor voice: This is so typical of American acting. You don't understand my talent. I am much deeper than this. I refuse to do it."

"Gee," I responded, "I thought you came to my class to grow and step out of your comfort zone."

Lee shot back, "You think you know everything."

"No. But I do know that all drama has comedy in it. All comedy has drama in it. We need both for the core of all forms of art, which mask human behavior."

He did it begrudgingly, without investing, to prove his point that comedy was a waste. Lee stayed in the role of Persecutor, because he didn't want to be judged. His fear of being found out that he was as broken as everyone else kept him apart from the group and didn't allow his authentic self to come through.

I let him see that the vulnerability was there, that even in comedy one could find meaning and be fascinated by it. That opened Lee up and he began to drop his armor, allowing me to guide him toward using his own delicious charm in comedy slices. He eventually revealed that the only way to survive around his father's dynamics while growing up was to be strong and not show his vulnerability.

After watching the videotaped playback of his classwork, Lee understood what I had been hoping to show him for the previous year. He realized that leaning on the Persecutor had not served him in any way. From that day on, Lee was open to creating different genres without labeling them. He understood that everything an actor does is an opportunity to live another person's life without judgment. Lee became a happier person, and that meant the most to me.

✳ Escape from the Triangle ✳

The way out of the triangle is first to acknowledge that the triangle even exists. Be aware of how easy it is to fall into one of the three roles: Victim, Rescuer, or Persecutor. This is a great place to apply the S-T-O-P method: Stop. Take a breath. Observe (yourself and your response), and Proceed when you can fully be the Adult (see chapter 1 for more information).

The Adult allows us to accept reality and lower our expectations. Be willing to change it and accept the outcome. For example: unless someone asks for help, I'm not going to burden him or her with my self-righteousness.

PREFERENCES—WHAT DO YOU MEAN, YOU DON'T TAKE CASH?

Acceptance of reality is the key to happiness.

My wife, Susan, and I were trapped in the exit lane of a mall parking lot. I couldn't find my credit card, and they wouldn't accept cash. The parking attendant refused to open the gate, and I couldn't back up because there were cars behind me.

The situation triggered Susan's anxiety, and finally, the gate guard let us out. As I turned the corner, I pulled over. "I left my credit card on the table at the restaurant," I told Susan. "I have to go back." Now, visibly losing it, Susan demanded to go home. Until that moment, I thought I was doing pretty well, not going into the role of Victim or Persecutor. But then I cracked. I started living in Susan's mess. My preference was that Susan not be anxious, but that wasn't happening.

It is easy for our preferences to get in the way, particularly when we are fighting with our significant other. *Why the hell can't Susan calm down? She's driving me crazy.* This is a statement of how I would prefer her behavior to be. Instead of locking onto preferences, what other options do I have? I can take a few deep breaths and shift

Deep Breath

my focus to anything that will break the connection, which will distract me from this tense interaction. I will give her a loving choice. "I'm happy to take an Uber. Would you like to take the car?"

Susan decided to wait in the car. When I returned from the restaurant with my credit card, I built on the momentum that began when I decided not to lock in on preferences. I vowed to myself to be even kinder, warmer, and more loving to Susan. It was a huge weight that was lifted off me.

As I drove home, I said, "It must be very hard to live in that space of anxiety."

She sighed. "I am so glad someone understands."

My default is now kindness, warmth, love, and wisdom, which replace any anger and defensiveness. It gets me out of the triangle. There is no safe place in the triangle. You never feel secure there.

MARGISM: ESCAPE THE TRIANGLE

I don't have to participate in every argument.

I can quiet my internal dialogue.

I can detach with love.

I can answer with compassion instead of taking the bait.

Paul's Story— "I Can't Stand…"

Margie was asked to do a workshop at our brokerage company to help our staff find their personal power. One of the exercises was to role play with anyone who was challenging and recreate the situation. I shared some of the problems I had with my boss, and we began the exercise.

ME
(Knocks on the door) May I come in?

MARGIE
(Without looking at me, she waves me in and says abruptly)
Come in. Come in.

ME
(Margie is still not looking at me, and I start to feel upset)
Here are the new market predictions you requested.

MARGIE
I don't have time to look at them. Just leave them on my
desk.

ME
(My thoughts are spinning with self-pity. I want to say: "You
told me to come in, and I have worked all night to get these
graphs done. How dare you be so mean? I hate working for
you." Instead, I said nothing.)

MARGIE
(Still not looking at me, which was really getting me mad) I'm
on a deadline here. Anything else?

ME
(My brain was filled with every curse word I knew) No. I'll
leave you to it.

I was so glad that "scene" was over. It felt excruciatingly real. We
talked about the feelings and thoughts I experienced during that
exercise. Margie explained I was stuck in the Victim part of the triangle. We had taped the simulated conversation, and it showed me
how my body language was slumped over like an unloved child with
a pouting face. I hadn't realized how those victim thoughts affected

my physical behavior. But I wasn't ready to let go of my preference. I protested: "I can't stand being treated like I am unimportant and inconsequential. I can't stand how he ignores me."

Margie said that thinking or articulating Victim thoughts puts you under the bus. It's preference-based. It's ego. It's constricting. First, you need to be aware of them. Then, take action that will enable you to shift out of the triangle to your Adult and be your kind, loving self.

Margie suggested that we do the "scene" again. "This time, I will be you, and you can be your boss. See what happens when you change your mindset from feeling sorry for yourself to being curious and empathetic as to what is going on in the heart and mind of the other person."

MARGIE (AS ME)
(Knocks on the door) May I come in?

ME (AS THE BOSS)
(Without looking at "me," I wave "me" in and say abruptly) Come in. Come in.

MARGIE (AS ME)
(Thinking the "boss" must be very busy) Here are the new market prediction graphs you asked for.

ME (AS THE BOSS)
I don't have time to look at it. Just leave it on my desk.

MARGIE (AS ME)
(Validating) I can see I caught you at a bad time. I'm happy to come back later.

ME (AS THE BOSS)
(Appreciative, with a deep breath) Thanks for understanding. I've had a splitting headache all day.

MARGIE (AS ME)
(Kindly) I get it. I'll leave you to it.

"OMG! How powerful did that feel? You stopped making it about yourself and brought out your strong, empathetic self," said Margie, cheering.

I responded, "It was great getting out of that Victim role." I gained back my power, and I walked away standing tall.

It seems my heart is made of tissue paper: I wish the world would handle it more delicately.

—Richelle E. Goodrich, author

SURVIVING EYE ROLLS

I have a friend who has been in my life for decades. When I am around her, I want her to see me. In typical Margie fashion, I walk into the room and take up too much space, hoping she'll notice me. Instead she often rolls her eyes at my attempts to be seen. Out pops my Victim, *She is so mean to me. Why doesn't she love me?*

I had the opportunity to finally meet my friend's father, and I was taken aback by his critical attitude toward his own daughter. I was then overcome with empathy for my friend and realized her behavior had nothing to do with me. From that point on, I stopped taking it personally. One day, she came over to help move my dining room table for a party. I saw her roll her eyes, because I wasn't doing it the way she thought I should. I smiled and moved away. I removed myself from the triangle! I didn't need to be a Victim of her behavior. I didn't need to Rescue her or find a reason to Persecute her. I just gently gave her room. I allowed the Adult in me to take the steering wheel, and you know how that turns out.

BUT I DID SUCH A GOOD JOB. NOTICE ME!

I love my sisters. They are amazing people, and everyone envies our relationship. Joan is a fabulous travel agent, and Lois is a fabulous mother who also works with Joan. Their teamwork has allowed my family to travel to many remarkable places around the world. We took a marvelous cruise through Italy and Spain with all the nieces, nephews, and cousins. As soon as I came home, I began the monumental task of creating a video and editing the thousand pictures down to 250. I spent weeks prioritizing this project. I proudly sent the finished video to my sisters. The reaction I received was not what I expected. Joan's first comment was that there were very few pictures of her, and Lois's reaction was that she preferred an album, not a video.

Here is how it went down for me in this famous triangle:

- Rescuer: I am going to make this great video for my whole family. They will love it, and they will love me so much for it, and I will be seen as special in their eyes. I am going to work very hard on it, so I can get it done by Lois's birthday. I will be the hero of our trip.
- Victim: I can't believe I sent it to them and haven't heard anything! How could they do that to me after all the work I put into it? Can't they show their appreciation by saying, "Margie, it is fantastic! You are so special! We love you so much!!" I am so hurt.
- Persecutor: How dare they treat me that way! Screw them! I'm never going to do anything for them again. And I'm not going to answer the phone when they call me. Or

call them back. It's their fault that I am so hurt. They deserve my anger.

The triangle robbed me of being the lead in my own life. It took away my power. When I was in a Rescuer role, I thought I was doing something beautiful, but it came with conditions and expectations. They have to behave a certain way, or I am not happy. I believe that I knew I was being a Victim, but I wasn't willing to let it go. Somehow being a Victim filled me up, and I felt less empty. I also wanted to be right, which caused me to become the Persecutor of my sisters. I realized I would have been so much happier if I could have just given that gift without any strings attached. They are both beautiful people whom I adore more than anyone can imagine. Now I can let go of judgment and just love them. Such a relief!

> Don't Take Anything Personally.
> Nothing others do is because of you.
> When you are immune to the opinions
> and actions of others, you won't be
> the victim of needless suffering.
>
> —Don Miguel Ruiz, author

THE "I" MESSAGE

You would be surprised how changing one little word can transform your communication. When our feelings get hurt, we have a tendency to be reactive. "You just yelled at me. What is wrong with you?" The listener feels attacked and will most likely respond in a similar tone. You are back in the triangle. But by replacing "you" with "I," magic happens. For example—"I get scared when I get yelled at."

This sentence expresses my feelings without blame. It is sharing without attacking. Now the listener feels empathy for your feelings because you have removed the listener from the equation.

Sometimes, we combine both the "I" message and the "you" message. This approach might seem harmless, but nothing can be further from the truth. "I am so angry because *you* yelled at me." In that tense moment, the "you" invalidates the "I." Instead, one could say, "I lashed out because *I* felt extremely insecure." The "I" message allows us to own our feelings and take responsibility for our actions.

Studio Focus: Conversations from the Classroom
WHAT MAKES YOU A DRAMA QUEEN?

INT. CLASSROOM—DAY

MARGIE
What makes you a Drama Queen? How and where do you get stuck in the triangle?

ALEX
Okay, I had a situation where my sisters and I had a falling out years ago. By the way, I will never speak to them the same way again.

MARGIE
Persecutor . . .

ALEX
Well, I fundamentally will never.
The class laughs along with Alex.
But seriously, my dad calls and tells me I should respond to one of my sister's texts, which immediately brought everything back. And I couldn't stop thinking about it for days. I felt unheard by my dad and not loved.

MARGIE

So, your Drama Queen is when you don't let go. Not being able to let go makes you a Victim, and you start to become a Persecutor by cutting them out of your life.

Margie turns to look at another student.

Chris?

CHRIS

I'm generally more of a Rescuer. I'm a fixer and try to solve things really fast, but put me in a car, and all that changes. I go into that triangle like nobody's business. I don't care if you're eighty-five. I will be ruthless. I can take those speed bumps and make them into a giant mountain.

MARGIE

It's the little things in life that aggravate us.

Margie looks at Amelia.

AMELIA

I'm a bit of a Victim. About a month ago, my mom sent me a text message saying that she loved me, and she's so sorry she never said it earlier. I didn't speak to her for seven years. I was on my own. I was sixteen.

A few students gasp.

MARGIE

When a child doesn't feel loved, it's always a climb up that mountain of feeling you're not worthy. As children, where do we get the love we need? We hope from our mom and dad. It makes us feel stronger. It gives us more power. So, the fact that she is now giving it to you at this age changes your script. What a great opportunity. You don't have to fall back into the Victim role.

AMELIA

I got to a point where I could empathize, but I still couldn't really forgive her.

MARGIE

It's great that you found your empathy. Give yourself a break. It takes time to forgive. What about you, Irina?

IRINA

Drama Queen—of course, I'm from Russia. It's in our blood. It's a grand tradition.

Class laughs.

And the ones who feel my wrath the most are the people closest to me.

MARGIE

What about you, Tyler?

TYLER

Growing up, I was the reliable one. When my family fell apart, I held everything together. I had a couple of friends come stay with me in high school 'cause their parents kicked them out. And what that got me was, "Tyler's a nice person." I crave that praise. The problem is, I give so much that when I don't get what I expect, I go into Persecutor. I go silent. I stop communicating altogether.

MARGIE

Expectations destroy relationships. It's all about communication and being kind to you. Cultivate self-fullness, not selfishness. How about you, Dakota?

DAKOTA

I definitely ping-pong between the Victim and the Persecutor. Not the Victim that says, "Everything happens to me," but with a sense of cynicism and negativity. When I can't take it anymore, either I'm consumed with rage, or I drop off the face of the earth.

MARGIE

The triangle bleeds through every aspect of our lives. When you do it in one area, it usually ends up happening in other areas too. It's so subtle in a lot of ways.

BETSY

I'm very hard on myself to the point where I've had people close to me say, "If you're hard on all these situations, I can only imagine how hard you're being on yourself." They think they are helping me with constructive criticism.

MARGIE

Beware of constructive criticism. It's bullshit. When you give that kind of criticism to somebody, you're telling that person what you think he or she needs to do. I have worked hard to embrace my Adult. Each time I act like an Adult is a small victory that ultimately leads to more joy. Getting out of that triangle frees me to be the best Margie. Stepping out of the triangle allows you to be the lead in your life.

POWER CHALLENGE

- In which part of the triangle do you unconsciously spend the most time—Victim, Persecutor, or Rescuer? Write down three examples of when you were stuck in it.
- Recall a time when you shifted roles in the triangle. Where did you start—Victim, Persecutor or Rescuer, and where did you end? How would it have been different if you had responded as the Adult?
- Have you ever played the blame game? Describe when you blamed someone else for a problem that you may have created.
- When helping others, are you more like a tugboat or a lighthouse? If you do get messy like a tugboat when trying to "save" others, write down ways to change your behavior to be more like a lighthouse.
- If you no longer have a preference for how you want your loved one to behave, could that actually empower and enrich

the relationship and make you happier? Think of a loved one and list three preferences you have. Read each one out loud and let it go.

- If oversensitivity is a source of suffering, where in your life does this apply? Describe two incidents where you were oversensitive and reacted as a victim. Now write two alternatives to those victim reactions.

- Let's practice "I" messaging. Look back at an argument where you used the word "you." In the movie of your life, rewrite the dialogue from that tumultuous scene using the "I" message.

4

Does Your Armor Serve You?

We humans are fragile. Our core is soft and messy and deeply complicated. It is sticky with fear, pain, sadness, and love. So, it is not surprising that we seek to cover it with a mask of humor, anger, or indifference. We are so afraid of being hurt that we have mastered the art of protecting ourselves. Often the mask that we think works best for us is like steel armor that wraps around our core so tightly that nothing can penetrate. What we used to protect us now imprisons us.

These masks can be helpful and also healthy as long as they are made of gauze, allowing some of the core to seep through. As people with many layers, we often don't realize when our masks stop serving us.

✳ Mask of Humor ✳

THE GREAT MAYA ANGELOU

The award-winning poet Maya Angelou was intimately familiar with how laughter could become a suit of armor against the world.

One poem describes a Black maid who works for a white family and uses humor to get through her workday. Maya set the scene. "You might think she's laughing, but she wasn't laughing. She was simply extending her lips and making a sound—ha, ha, ha." Maya Angelou performed her impression of the Black maid's laugh with tears pouring out of her eyes.

Maya Angelou personally understood the pain and sadness of her own core. It was the mask of laughter that protected Black women from their deep pain and tears.

Studio Focus: Conversations from the Classroom
KEEPING EVERYTHING LIGHT

INT. CLASSROOM—DAY

MARGIE
All of us use different masks to protect our vulnerable selves. I use humor. Who wants to start?
There's a bit of hesitation around the room. Beat.
  Sarah raises her hand.

SARAH
I'll say the same as you: humor. It's using the lens that pretends that everything is great.

MARGIE
Keeping life light.

SARAH
Yes! It's always: "Sarah's here, the party is starting," or "Sarah's here, and we'll have fun now." It feels good, so I play it up. I hide my true feelings. I don't show all of myself. I've gotten feedback from casting, "We don't see Sarah quite that vulnerable." So, I know that's something I need to look at.

MARGIE

Knowing yourself well gives you personal power. Your job is to look at when humor doesn't serve you in your own life. We do need masks. We talk in class about how the core comprises your feelings of sadness, pain, fear, and love. And sometimes we reduce the thickness of our masks when we're with the people we trust.

Chris imitates Goofy, the animated dog.

CHRIS

Definitely, humor is a big mask for me.

MARGIE

Ya think?!

CHRIS

(Settling down)

It's always been a defense mechanism. I'll do something silly, hoping that maybe you'll just look at that, and I won't have to expose my true feelings.

MARGIE

It fascinates me that the mask of humor can be so appreciated by so many people that we don't want to lose that reward. Will I still be lovable without it? For many of us, it's a huge risk.

All the things I really like to do are either immoral, illegal, or fattening.

—Alexander Woollcott, drama critic

Tiffany Haddish's Story—
"Just Let Me Do My Thing!"

The day I walked into Margie's class, I knew she wasn't going to let me get away with anything. It was a vulnerable time. I didn't want anyone to know that I had been living in my car—homeless. But I was determined to study and become a better actor. I only wanted to do comedy, but Margie had other ideas for me. She wanted me to dive into my core of pain and sadness. I said: "Why would I do that? I want to make people laugh. There's too much pain in there to touch. I'm staying away from it."

Margie explained that all human beings are layered. Comedy has drama, and drama has comedy. "Okay," Margie said. "Here is a comedy slice. Spend some time creating it and look for what is underneath it."

When I was finished, Margie created the same slice but as a drama. I was surprised to see how much more core Margie discovered under the mask of humor. Then, she asked me to stand up. With empathy, she asked me about my childhood. At first, I deflected the question with my usual "shtick" and tried to "tap dance" my way out of it.

But that girl just won't let you get away with it! She wrapped her arms around me, repeating: "You are safe. No one is going to hurt you. You are safe. No one's going to hurt you. You are safe."

My armor cracked. My tears were like acid stripping away my walls. I trusted Margie. I shared my life in foster families and all the abuse. She hugged me and whispered, "You are loved. Do the slice again." This time, I started out looking at the truth of my character's life and then covered it with humor. After Margie filmed it, I watched the tape. I had to admit it was damn good.

I learned from Margie that there are different types of comedy— some have more reality than others. But there are "slices" where I could be more vulnerable and survive. That began a new path of openness.

When the walls came down, I had a revelation. Everything that I have been through, everything that I have suffered, all the adversity could actually serve me now as an artist. By tapping into it, I could enrich and expand my creativity. It's so powerful!

> *A good laugh heals a lot of hurts.*
>
> —Madeleine L'Engle, author

* Mask of Anger *

Anger is a healthy mask when you remove the smoke and fire of self-righteousness. It is unhealthy when it is dumped onto the listener. Often, we want to make the other person feel as bad as we feel. Anger can wipe out any chance of connection if it comes from an immediate, reactive, poisonous place. The pain is so deep that instead of taking responsibility for our part, we resort to the blame game. It is just so much easier. But if we truly want happiness, then we need to risk being vulnerable and remove the steel protection. *Do I want to win, or do I want to communicate?*

Studio Focus: Conversations from the Classroom
WHY THE FUCK AM I SO ANGRY?

INT. CLASSROOM—DAY

MARGIE

People end up using anger as a way to protect themselves. There's humor and there's indifference, but anger is a very special armor to which many of us cling tightly. When anger gets out of control, it can stop the relationship from being healthy. Do you use anger as a way to protect yourself?

MELANIE

The only time that I use anger, which is interesting, is with my wife. Every other person, I don't. My wife plows full steam ahead, which shuts us both down. Anger is bad stuff.

MARGIE

Well, anger isn't always bad, you know? It is an accepted feeling when communicated cleanly, without the desire to annihilate your listener. It's when it becomes a weapon to retaliate that it gets us in trouble. Then anger becomes armor.

MELINA

I feel like my life has been a master class of this because I'm Greek, and it's just me and my mom and my sister. I recently discovered we very much use it as armor, and I think I'm kind of breaking out of it a bit, because I see how unhealthy it is. But my mother and sister still can press those buttons. There's very much a "shutting off" of the conversation. They'll tell me that I'm getting aggressive, and I don't admit it, but I am. I realize I'm aggressive out of fear of not being understood, or "we're drifting apart because of this." If we aren't in harmony, it's very scary, because all we have is one another.

MARGIE

When you love somebody so much, anger is the easiest way to protect yourself. It can get hardened with self-righteousness until it turns into armor, and you have no way of getting rid of it.

AMY

I definitely use anger as armor. I often use it as a protection to stop from crying. After my anger tantrums, I usually cry.

RICHARD

My anger usually starts out unconsciously. Then, when I realize what I'm doing, I become aware of what's underneath it—my fear or sadness. Sometimes I'll just jump to it as a default instead of really expressing myself. I've gotten better at catching myself, because it doesn't work to come at each other like that.

MARGIE

Yes. The relationship suffers. You have to, at that moment, notice it, breathe, and realize that you don't have to be controlled by your anger. It's a bad habit. Did you want to say something, Kimberley?

KIMBERLEY

I think a lot of people don't have the skills for conflict resolution. I don't think anger is a bad thing. I think it's definitely necessary, especially if you're defending yourself. And I have, like, a little "Joe Pesci" that lives inside of me. "Get me angry in the street, and I'll get scrappy." My friend started yelling at me, and I had to stop her and say, "If you want me to be the villain, I will be." And her retort was, "Why aren't you fighting with me?" I think some people don't know how to work things out. I think it's a skill we all need to develop.

MARGIE

I think there's a difference between expressing your anger directly rather than being accusatory.

MELANIE

I get angry with people I care about. If I don't care about them, then I'm just like, "Oh, fuck it, it's just not worth the energy."

MARGIE

Cary and Tyler, because you are such sweet men, do you ever get really angry, or are you afraid of your anger and go to rage? Cary?

CARY

I can get very angry. Usually, I'm really good at *almost* getting angry when something bothers me. And then I stop, and I take a breath and another breath, and then I'll never do anything about it.

MARGIE

Anger is healthy if it's direct anger. Tyler?

TYLER

I had a lot of trouble with anger growing up. I actually had to go to anger management in the fourth grade. So, from my experience with that, I would say that I tend to shy away from anger more because I'm afraid if I get angry, it will go to rage, and then I can't control myself.

CARY

I'm very intrigued by Tyler's rage.

TYLER

It doesn't happen often, but when it does, it's not pretty.

MARGIE

It must be difficult for both you and Cary. I have been watching you both grow. You are finding this incredible power in stepping out of your comfort zone and into a world you previously avoided. To further this cause, change your relationship with anger. You don't have to run away from it. If you give yourself permission to be angry, then you wouldn't be so afraid of it. Be direct without blame. You might find it will become a positive tool that will end up serving you.

Anger is as a stone cast into a wasp's nest.

—Pope Paul VI

Bobby's Story—
Hercules

B obby was a student of mine. He had what some people might think was a perfect body for a man—if you like muscles. He was my Hercules. But the muscles were his armor. Bobby didn't like to talk about feelings and didn't share much of himself. It was hard to get Bobby angry about anything.

I decided to do the back-to-back exercise and volunteered Bobby. Most of the time, the exercise is done with a man and a woman, but if I am lucky, I get to put two men together. I asked Bobby to sit on the floor behind another guy in the class, back to back.

In his nonconfrontational way, he quietly said, "I'm not comfortable sitting behind a guy like that."

I replied: "This is an opportunity for you. Please get up and do the exercise."

Begrudgingly Bobby took his place behind his classmate with his "scene" on his lap. I set up the situation by telling them that they were brothers, and they hadn't seen each other for a while. I instructed them in this exercise not to rush to the paper to respond. I wanted them to experience the voice and the other parts of their partner before picking up their lines.

At first, we could see how uncomfortable Bobby was by the rigidity of his back and how he worried about the lines. I asked them both to imagine they were young boys playing on a seesaw, pushing and pulling, back and forth, back and forth. As they got into it, Bobby started having fun and took his focus off his uncomfortable position. Both boys were competitive and wanted to win so much that they pushed hard, landing straight on their backs with each one's head resting on the other's shoulders. I told them to connect with their breath and stay in that place for a while. They were so close together that both of their faces were only separated by a fraction. I asked them to close their eyes. They could feel the other person's chest moving and their heart palpitating. They both began to relax and enjoy being in the moment.

I then whispered to Bobby: "I want you to imagine you are next to the most important male in your life. Whisper in his ear whatever you need to say or never had a chance to say." The room was still; I could hear everyone's breath sighing at the same time in anticipation of what would come next. Bobby brought his lips to his partner's ear and whispered something that we could not hear. His partner took it in, paused, and did the same.

Bobby surprised all of us as he lovingly touched his partner's head. Then it was as if an ominous black cloud released rain from Bobby's eyes that flooded from his soul. He cried and cried as his partner held him tight. It took everything we had as an audience not to get up there and hold him as well. Finally, when the cloud seemed to be emptied and a light appeared on Bobby's face, I asked them both to sit up. They were reluctant to let each other go and sat up glued to each other.

I asked him if he was willing to share the experience.

He nodded. "When you said to me to put someone next to me, I chose my father. My dad was an alcoholic. I grew up never feeling safe, never knowing which father would come home. When he was good, he was good, and when he was bad, he was horrible. When I was ten, he beat my mom so badly that she had to go to the hospital. I had tried to stop him, but he was too strong, too big. We had restraining orders to protect us, but I never felt safe. Eventually, my father got help and got clean and spent years trying to make it up to me, but I was too filled with hate. He died alone. When my mom died, I held her in my arms, and she made me promise never to be angry again. So, that's what I did. I buried my anger."

"So, Bobby," I asked, "What did you whisper to your partner?"

Bobby looked straight at me as the tears swelled up his eyes and softly said, "I forgive you."

I had never seen such a transformation so quickly. Then I went up and hugged the two boys, and everyone else in the class followed me, ready to give them the love they had to share. Bobby changed after that and became more vulnerable.

Years later, I was talking about that incident involving this muscular guy to my new ongoing group, when a man raised his hand and said: "That was me. I was that guy."

I didn't recognize him because he was small and lean.

Bobby explained, "When I left your class, I realized how I was using those muscles to protect me. I needed them for my father, and I promised my mom that I would never be angry, so the muscles were my way of holding on to all those feelings. Every time you gave me 'a slice of life' where I had to be angry, I was stuck in fear of it. When I forgave my father, I was able to forgive myself and understand that it was okay to be angry."

I seriously didn't recognize him. I was so moved that he had gone on such a great journey, only to return with so much power. He didn't need the muscles anymore. He wasn't afraid of his father's anger or his own.

Anger is an acid that can do more harm
to the vessel in which it is stored than
to anything on which it is poured.

—Mark Twain, author

✳ Mask of Indifference ✳

The definition of indifference is "something you neither like nor dislike." It doesn't have to have an emotion connected to it. Take it or leave it. For example, a mom asks her child whether she wants aspar-agus or spinach for the dinner vegetable, and the girl responds, "I don't care, either one." This is an honest response of indifference.

As a mask, indifference may not be as harmless. It is used as a means of protection to keep us from being hurt. But it is not authen-tic. There may not be any argument. Everything may seem okay on the surface, but underneath the words of indifference is a much stronger emotion. Perhaps you are stewing with resentment, which is destroying the joy of the relationship.

Rosie's Story— Whatever

I use "whatever" a lot when I don't want someone to know I'm upset or hurt. I tend to mutter under my breath, "whatever," and the true thoughts follow silently with either, *I am so pissed off*, or *How dare she?* On the outside, it looks like I'm indifferent, but it is totally the opposite on the inside.

I'm a workaholic. I am obsessed with getting things done and doing them right. I had a meeting at my office with my boss and two other colleagues. I was to give a presentation to clients the follow-ing day. It was a complicated talk, and I really wanted to make this meeting short. My boss threw a wrench into my plans when he said, "I know you are working on this project alone, but I would like John to help you so it can also come from a male point of view."

In my mind, certainly not out loud, I screamed: *Are you kidding me? I have spent days working on this presentation, and you want to bring in a male perspective! This is so typical of how men think women are second-class citizens and that we are not capable of understanding both male and female customers!* But instead of showing any signs of my outrage, I put on a mask and mumbled under my breath, "Whatever."

"Whatever" was my giant shield. I did not want anyone in that room to know how terribly hurt I was, so I covered it with indifference. The problem is that pain doesn't go away. It remains hidden behind the shield, gnawing away at me.

Studio Focus: Conversations from the Classroom
I'M BOILING A POT OF WATER INSIDE MY BODY

INT. CLASSROOM–DAY

JAMES
I think I avoid anger by being indifferent. I use the words, "It's okay."

MARGIE
Indifference is the mask on top of the anger. It's like an artichoke with its points clipped to prevent it from pricking you, but underneath is the hardness of the leaves that is the anger protecting the heart of the artichoke.

JAMES
That is exactly what it feels like. My wife is nagging me, and I don't want to get into a fight, so I have an attitude of "I don't care." I refuse to let her in and make my day miserable.

MARGIE
It's amazing how much power we give to our loved ones when we don't want to go there. You know it will come out sooner or later.

PAM
That's what happens with my teenager. He rattles on about how he is going to run away if I don't cut him some slack, so I

casually go, "Do it if it is going to make you happy." Of course, I am far from calm inside. I just look like I am in a state of meditation. (I wish!)

MARGIE

My son can easily get me there. I, too, try to mask my pain and anger with indifference, but he can read right through me. He called to tell me he wasn't coming over that day as planned. I hadn't seen him for weeks. My response to his call was: "No problem. See you next week." Truth be known, I was boiling a pot of water inside my body.

Indifference and neglect often do much more damage than outright dislike.

—J.K. Rowling, author, in *Harry Potter and the Order of the Phoenix*

* The Cultural Mask of Polite Distance *

Sometimes, it is not fear that stops us from opening up, but the culture we have been brought up in, a societal climate that forbids anyone to complain or express fears. As the British would say, "Stiff upper lip."

Brooke Williams's Story— "What School Did You Go To?"

grew up in Christchurch, a small city on the South Island of New Zealand. It's prim and proper, conservative, white, and repressed, with a seething underbelly of dark and graphic violence. Class is a big deal in Christchurch. The British influence leads to the commonly asked question to ascertain social standing, "What school did you go to?" It's a weird kaleidoscope of contradictions and displacement. The common mask is polite distance.

Feelings are embarrassing, individuality is very embarrassing, and bodies are very embarrassing.

I went to strict private schools. My dad was a builder, and he and my mum worked their asses off to send me there. I remember being so confused that the other girls' dads had hands that were soft and smelled of cologne, not sawdust and metal and sweat.

I liked school, but individuality was definitely not encouraged. Creativity was only encouraged within very narrow parameters. There was a lot of shame-based punishment. I was a timid kid anyway, and I pretty much didn't speak for the first two years of school for fear I might say something wrong or stupid and have to stand up in front of the assembly and have a house point deducted. I was acutely aware at five that I was different.

I got into acting as an escape and because I wanted people to listen to me. I got so tired of my tiny voice being trod over all the time, but when I was on stage, and everyone was sitting in their seats in the dark, and I had the light on me, they *had* to listen. I loved and craved being able to express big things—feelings that would be shamed by others if they came from me, Brooke, in real life. If I expressed them through a character's life, people would literally applaud me for it. But they were my feelings all along, and my depth and darkness were channeled through a filter of a person with a different name and different experiences. It felt like a secret, like something I was getting away with, and I adored it.

Elizabeth's Story— White Glove Syndrome

I grew up in a rich family. I remember our dinner table. The butler and the cook would make sure all the silver was polished. My mom had a buzzer under her foot when she needed something from the kitchen. My siblings and I were given elocution lessons. "How now brown cow" was a phrase used to help us with our diction. Politeness was part of respect. Though we had an enormous amount of love, I never saw my parents angry. "Not in front of the kids" was how my parents behaved to avoid showing conflict and strong negative emotions around their children. They were unacceptable.

When we were angry, no one was to know about it. It didn't make a difference how upset we were—we did not share feelings. Let everyone on the outside assume you have a perfect life. I remember coming home from school to find that my younger brother had ripped my science project to pieces. My parents immediately instructed me not to be angry. "He didn't mean it. He's just a baby. Don't be angry." I didn't get to express my anger as it was considered improper, and I learned to bury it out of guilt for even feeling it.

FEMALE POWER

On my way to my studio one morning, I got a call from Laurie, an executive at a large insurance company.

"I heard you're an acting coach who helps people remove their walls and share vulnerability," Laurie said. "We want to hire you to work with the women in our company. There is a lack of openness and vulnerability with our female employees, very little interaction.

Everyone stays to herself, and no one seems to want to step out of her comfort zone."

After talking to a few of the executives at the company, we decided I would start with one big kickoff meeting with three hundred women, then ten days of smaller breakout sessions of thirty women in each, focusing on female leadership.

In the large gathering, I could sense that their overall perspective was the typical "I'm a woman in a male-dominated business" belief. I started with a listening exercise to connect them to one another. Then, I wrote three words on the board: Define female power.

Under it, I wrote their answers:

- Control
- Strong
- Decisive
- Intelligent
- Confident
- Authoritative

Almost everyone thought it was important to give the appearance that you had it all together. It was clear that they felt they had to wear armor to survive.

Ironically, the words above were mostly masculine.

I wrote the following words to describe female power:

- Curious
- Empathetic
- Vulnerable
- Passionate
- Open

It seemed clear that most of the three hundred women thought control and wearing armor were powerful, and being vulnerable and open were weak.

I asked them who they thought was a powerful woman. Some said Hillary Clinton, because they thought she was tough and strong. It is interesting that many of my friends have met Hillary and found her to be full of humor and vulnerability, contrary to her public persona.

In the next five days, the women were organized into smaller groups. Most of these women had worked with one another for a long time, but knew very little about their colleagues. I've worked with many corporate companies where this is the norm. I did an exercise in the smaller groups where they sat on the floor sharing their childhood memories. Some were willing to go there. Others were afraid to be judged.

One woman angrily retorted, "This isn't appropriate for a workplace."

I touched her shoulder and gently guided her: "It's okay. I'm here for you."

Soon, her armor cracked, and her tears rolled down her cheeks. She shared her truths, and her vulnerability allowed others to do the same. At the end of the day, instead of rushing out the door, everyone stayed for hours, drinking wine, laughing, and genuinely connecting with one another. The shields were down, and my job was done. It was beautiful.

> *Politeness is one-half good nature*
> *and the other half good lying.*

—Mary Wilson Little, author, *A Paragrapher's Reveries* (1904)

✳ Masking Without Armor ✳

CARING WITH BOUNDARIES

I was teaching in Atlanta. It was a wonderful, loving group, and one of those kind students volunteered to take me to my niece Jennifer's home at the end of the day. During the thirty-minute drive, he shared his appreciation for the opportunity to be so open and so validated. Though he and his wife were divorced, they still lived together, and he slept on the couch, never feeling strong enough to leave. He spent the rest of our journey to my niece's place describing his failed marriage.

Once we arrived, I introduced Jennifer to my student. He began to cry as he shared how much he loved the workshop and me. I took a breath and hugged him as he wept in my arms. I noticed my niece covering up her own tears.

When my student left, I told Jennifer, "I'm so sorry he made you cry."

Jennifer replied, "I wasn't crying over him. I was crying over seeing you care about him while at the same time maintaining your boundaries."

I smiled and gave her credit: "I can stay loving and still be self-contained, because I use the image of the iridescent bubble that you shared with me."

Jennifer had told me that, as an empath, she would take on all emotions—good and bad—sadness, anger, pain, love, and fear. To live a balanced life, she found an image that supported her in being the lead in her own life.

Bubbles are iridescent, translucent, and beautiful. They ebb, flow, and flex. They're not rigid or inflexible. They are soft, organic, and approachable.

MARGISM: STEP INTO YOUR BUBBLE

When you're in a situation where you may need to protect yourself or are giving out too much of your energy to others, visualize a bubble surrounding you and creating a gentle boundary.

Breathe.

Pause.

Visualize your iridescent bubble.

Remember, every encounter is another opportunity for a small victory that helps you to be the lead in your own life.

> *People will throw stones at you.*
> *Don't throw them back.*
> *Collect them all and build an empire.*

—Anonymous

"STICKS AND STONES"

"Sticks and stones may break my bones, but words will never hurt me."

That expression was supposed to protect us from the arrows shot by mean children, bullies who send other children home in tears. The more I dive into knowing myself, the more I realize how over-sensitive I have been.

I grew up with unconditional love and never knew how to protect myself from the arrows of meanness shot at me. "Tough skin" was never developed. My skin can develop toughness if it's rubbed. "Your new haircut makes you look old" is a rub. It doesn't have to become a wound. The skin is an external organ. Feel the sting on your skin, but don't let the arrow pierce your heart. I have to let it bounce off of me. It was just an "ouch." I don't have to go to the emergency room. It doesn't have to go any further. I am the only one in charge of my sensitive feelings. I acknowledge that I am working on it. These are all bad habits. See it, accept it, and move away from it. I can take care of myself.

> *Trust yourself. You've survived a lot. You'll*
> *survive whatever is happening right now too.*

—Karen Salmansohn, author

Don't Fertilize Your Soil with Your Own Shit

MARGIE

I seem to have two ways to go down the road of anger. One is I clam up and stew; the other is I lash out. They're both really damaging to me and my relationships. I had been in that mode of letting it stew, but a few nights ago, I lashed out. My wife and I were watching television, and then we put it on pause to discuss our party that we were having this weekend. Because we're still in the COVID-19 pandemic, I expressed my fears and the need for boundaries—social distancing and wearing a mask. When I mentioned that I didn't want anyone to congregate around the food table, communication crumbled. Susan moaned: "You never trust me. Let me do it my way for a change."

THERAPIST

Go real slow right there.

MARGIE

My stomach churned and I didn't catch it. My response was: "Are you kidding me? I'm not going to have this party if you're not going to do it the way we discussed it. Okay?" Her retort, "Well, good, then we won't have it." I quickly removed myself from the living room to my bedroom to calm myself down because none of it was working well.

All of a sudden, it smelled like the pool water chlorine was penetrating the entire house. I was still angry, upset. And I'm trying to find out where this smell is coming from. Susan had poured an enormous amount of Clorox into the washing machine because she was freaking out about the dirt in the machine. I slammed the washer door saying: "Do you really not know by now how this smell destroys me? You know I'm allergic to it!" *Boom!* My anger was now rage. I went back into my room, slammed my door, and pouted.

THERAPIST

So, what was the source of this rage?

MARGIE

Thoughts that I'm going to get sick.

THERAPIST

I find it best to say "imagination."

MARGIE

My imagination went wild. "I'm going to get the virus, and I'm going to die." And I went down that rabbit hole. That's really the source that causes the anger to come out.

THERAPIST

What desire is being blocked or interfered with? You're not getting the safety protocol you want. You're not getting the cooperation you want to social distance at this party, period. Okay. That's easy to understand. It's that simple, right? Because that's what you're talking about, but then you both went cuckoo. Susan went first.

MARGIE

I attached myself to it.

THERAPIST

You've got to follow what you teach. S-T-O-P: Stop. Take a breath. Observe. Proceed.

MARGIE

I went to the reactive response immediately when I heard her go to her Victim response.

THERAPIST

What does that have to do with you?

MARGIE

Exactly.

THERAPIST

Let's be honest, though. When I'm with someone I love, and they go cuckoo on me, I can't play with them anymore. I'm not having fun. And I lose my playmate, my companion. I lose healthy normalcy, right?

MARGIE

So, I have to pivot and change the topic.

THERAPIST

You can diffuse the anger by saying, "I am so sorry I insinuated that this has anything to do with your competency, your love for me, and your ability to keep me safe." It's kind, and it's not necessary to be right. And that's why we have the word "righteous."

MARGIE

Righteous behavior.

THERAPIST

It's a different set of values. It's wanting to get along rather than being right. I want peace more than I want to be right.

MARGIE

Getting along is so much better than being right.

THERAPIST

Your reactions are bad habits. I'm always trying to get your space to be creative. Otherwise, you're just a reflex robot machine.

MARGIE

So, I need to be creative with my anger as well.

THERAPIST

Yes, and anger that is healthy is being clear. "You did X, and X is unacceptable." And you explain why.

MARGIE

So, healthy anger is saying, "I'm feeling very angry."

THERAPIST

Yeah. But did you see where my eyes and head pointed?

MARGIE

You didn't look directly at the person.

THERAPIST

Yeah, because then it's going to land on that person's body.

MARGIE

All right. So, when you're expressing things like anger or other feelings, it's best to face away from the person?

THERAPIST

Better to point it at the dirt. Don't fertilize the soil with your own shit. Don't throw your anger at someone or distort your body and face.

MARGIE

That's exactly the way I looked with the Clorox incident. I needed to ground myself and S-T-O-P time because I was enraged. I was past anger.

THERAPIST

You know, a yogic remedy for being enraged is to get an ice cube and touch all of the orifices. So, one, two, three, four, five, six, seven, eight, nine orifices.

MARGIE

The mouth, the nose, the ears, the vagina, and the eyes, et cetera, et cetera, et cetera.

THERAPIST

Or a cool pack, one of those gel packs. Yeah.

MARGIE

If I could get an ice-cold towel and put it on my different orifices, that calms the nervous system?

THERAPIST

Why do we have the expression, "You're so . . .?"

MARGIE

Hotheaded.

THERAPIST

And, "Will you cool down?" Rage damages the nervous system. Picture anger on a thermometer—rage is at the top. You're just playing with the temperature.

MARGIE

I needed to walk it off. Get a cold compress. Take a dip in the cool water of my pool.

I'm a victim of my own insides. It used to make me very unhappy, all that feeling. I just didn't know what to do with it. But now I've learned to make that feeling work for me.

—Janis Joplin, singer

✳ You're Only as Sick as Your Secrets ✳

Sometimes, when we do not address the pain and sadness that we are experiencing, the fear of exposing our vulnerability takes over, causing us to overprotect our core. We become entrapped by the false belief that we are dealing with our feelings. Then we wake up one day, and the secrets we are harboring take up too much space. It's then we need to make a choice. Will we step out of our comfort zone?

Margie's Story— Outing Myself

grew up using humor as a form of armor. I entertained everyone, and they all thought I was this adorable kid. What they didn't know is that my humor helped me hide all the fear I had inside—the fear of people knowing the secret I kept for decades.

I had my first crush on a camp counselor. Harriet was beautiful, and I followed her around like a little puppy dog, always hoping she would choose me to be on her team. I didn't know it then, but it was the first of many crushes on women that would eventually catapult me into a world of fear of being "found out."

In junior high, we moved to the Garden Apartments on a street named Broadway (only later in life did I realize how ironic it would be).

Carol was a young college graduate who lived next door. She looked like Elizabeth Taylor, and sometimes, when my parents went out late, I would stay at her house. We would have sleepover dates, and I would be so happy tickling her back. That was my secret life.

I knew I was different in high school. I had two boyfriends named David. I gave them the last name of the colleges they went to, David Colgate and David Harvard, to distinguish them. They were handsome and I felt pretty popular, but it was Judy (a high school senior) that I secretly had a crush on. In my long prom dress and my sixties flip hairdo, I danced all night with David Harvard, wishing it were Judy in my arms. No one knew the guilt I felt. In the sixties, being gay was perceived as a sickness. In my mind, only lesbians who looked like men were homosexuals. That wasn't me. I had long blond hair, wore makeup, and dated boys. I felt isolated and terrified, but I stuffed those feelings deep inside and continued my masquerade. I look back at these days with such compassion for that confused Margie, who had no one to talk to about her feelings and no one as a role model.

This secret life continued as I entered Ithaca College. I refused to even think about any crushes on girls and, by my sophomore year, was going steady with Sam Levy from Cornell University. I convinced myself that he was perfect for me—handsome, premed, fraternity guy, and Jewish!

Then, an adorable freshman girl came into my life. Jackie was a breath of fresh air—a smart, cute cheerleader type who was so much fun to be around and seemed to want to spend every second with me. It wasn't long before I realized she had an enormous crush on me, and I was feeling nervous just being in her presence. She was like my little puppy that sometimes could be annoying but was always adorable. My group of friends was very into playing canasta and bridge. Jackie would sit next to me while I played cards, and I began feeling this unfamiliar, hot energy going through my body whenever she would touch my hand or stay a little longer for the greeting or goodnight hugs.

I didn't know what to do with these troubling but titillating sensations. I was horrified. I wanted her to disappear and all the pain and fear along with it. Jackie became an addiction for me. I wanted Jackie to be with me all the time but pushed her away as much as I could. The whole sophomore year was a push/pull of agony and ecstasy. Jackie had no problem with the idea of having a woman as a lover. But I could not accept it. There had to be something fundamentally wrong with me. After all, I didn't look gay. I didn't act gay. So, how could I be gay? I was only familiar with the stereotypes.

Meanwhile, I was still going out with Sam. When he kissed me, I couldn't help but wonder what it would be like to kiss Jackie. In class, I would be writing *Levy* all over my notebooks, lost in my fantasy. Everyone thought I was dreaming of Sam Levy. No one knew it was Jackie Levy. How convenient for me that they both had the same last name. It must have been excruciating for Jackie. She knew what she wanted. My body and my heart said "yes"; my head said "no."

My group and I decided to take a vacation to the "Jewish Alps"—the Catskill Mountains. Jackie volunteered to be my roommate at the hotel. Of course, my friends did not know of the terrible guilty secret I kept within me, so I had to say yes. I had already pleaded with Jackie to change her mind and not come with us, but there was no way she wasn't going to take advantage of this opportunity.

I resigned myself to avoid her as much as possible, but it's hard to avoid one who is lying right next to me. Our backs were resting against each other. It felt like we were cradled in a bed of heat and sweat when Jackie turned her body toward me, removing her clothes and allowing her warm skin to touch mine. I was on fire, trying to resist every temptation as her fingers slid down my back. Jackie was gently turning me over to place her lips on mine when I freaked out and pushed her off the bed. I screamed at her: "This will never work. I cannot have you in my life. I won't allow myself to love a woman. It's sick!"

I saw Jackie on the ground with tears welling up and the pain of rejection covering her face. I knew I had hurt her for the last time. And I was right. Jackie didn't talk to me for the rest of our college years. I did see Jackie a few times, but each time I approached her, she ignored me, and it became abundantly clear that she had changed. She looked radically different from the "cheerleader girl" I had first met. She had become more of a "hippie." I felt such guilt for the pain I caused her and the shame I felt inside.

I hid the secret of my gay feelings from everyone except for a boy I met freshman year who was also obsessed with Judy Garland (that should give you a hint!). We were both petrified to share these feelings, afraid to find out if the other was suffering from the same shame. After "coming out," we became a lifeline for each other. Jeffrey and I were inseparable.

Jeffrey convinced me to spend the summer of 1967 singing and waiting on tables in the Catskills. We would sing at different hotels but stayed at the Shanks Hotel where we were waiters. (I have to say that was not my forte.) A funny, sarcastic girl, Lynn, from Long Island, was the receptionist. Lynn was the best. Then a handsome, dark-haired, six-feet-two, chiseled-face waiter named Ronald Eric Anderson from Detroit swept me off my feet. I couldn't believe it. Maybe I wasn't gay! That summer would change the direction of my life. Ronnie and I became lovers, and I was as happy as could be. Maybe he would change me? (My mom would say, "You just haven't met the right boy!" *Ugh*—it should be that simple!)

Ronnie was my boyfriend for the rest of the school year, but when he broke up with me, I was miserable and called my friend Lynn.

One evening, Lynn and I were on our way to a movie when I felt this familiar hot heat coming from Lynn's hand that was close to mine. I stopped breathing and noticed she looked paler than usual. We said nothing as we entered the theater and sat in our seats. The movie started, and our bodies got closer and closer until I thought they had raised the temperature in the theater to 100 degrees. We had no idea what the movie was about, only that we were attracted to each other.

Silently, we went back to her house where her parents lived and got into our single beds. I couldn't sleep. An hour later, I felt Lynn sitting at the end of my bed. I sat up staring at her beautiful blue eyes and her very soft lips (to this day, she is obsessed with lip balms, and I swear her lips melted because of it) reached mine. There was no way I could resist the feeling this time. We made love, and I had never felt so fulfilled. In the middle of our lustful affair, I returned to Ithaca to graduate and enrolled in Brooklyn Graduate School. All my friends thought I was still pining over Ronnie. Only Jeffrey knew my true despair, realizing that I am gay.

For the next year, Lynn and I became lovers. I lived with my parents, and my room shared their bedroom wall. We had to be very quiet, so most of the time, I would throw her into my closet (ironic) and we would make love on top of my shoes. It didn't make a difference to me. I was in love and had to have her. On the other hand, Lynn treated our relationship as if it was a normal friendship with the benefit of sex. She could see me only once a week, but I was obsessed and couldn't be without her. If she was five minutes late, I would get insanely impatient. Finally, it grew too much for her. She needed space. I was engulfing her, and she could no longer handle it and broke up with me. If I thought Ronnie was devastating, it paled in comparison to my torn heart after Lynn left. After all, if I was going to be gay, I wasn't going to treat it casually. I gave every part of myself and had nothing left.

The depth of the pain drove me to leave the East Coast, and in my late twenties, I ended up in California where I entered a long-term relationship with a woman named Pam. I kept this shameful secret, never telling anyone, even pretending to live in two separate rooms so the world would think we were just roommates.

In my midthirties, I realized I could not have a happy life without coming out to my parents. I flew to see them at their home in Florida. My sister, Lois, was visiting there at that time. I decided to take the risk of outing myself to her first and if that went well, then maybe I could proceed to the really difficult task of sharing it with my parents. Lois and I went out for a drink. (I must have had at least three J&B scotches on the rocks.) After much silence, I bravely told her that I was bisexual. I couldn't even say the word "gay" or that horrible word "lesbian."

Lois's reaction was simply, "We all assumed."

I gasped. "*We!?* Do you mean Mommy and Daddy?"

She said: "That is why I am out to dinner with you. They wanted me to find out the truth."

I thought I was going to pass out. Instead, I got drunk and managed to crawl my way into my parents' apartment. The next morning, I knew that I couldn't escape and that this was the moment of truth. I slowly walked out on the balcony, where my parents were seated, and to my surprise, blurted out, "I'm gay, I'm gay, I'm gay."

My mom said, "Shh, the neighbors," and we walked back into the den where I had been sleeping. Then she looked at me and said, "I don't want to talk about your dames."

Dames? *Dames?!* What was that? If I weren't so scared, I would have laughed at that very descriptive word!

She continued: "I don't want to talk about it. Go outside and play with the kids and your sister."

I felt like I was seven years old, being dismissed by the Queen. (We always treated her like a queen.)

My father, in his gentle, loving, innocent way, said: "Don't worry, darling, it's temporary. It's Hollywood."

After getting my bathing suit and stuff together, I passed the hall closet where my father was putting some clothes away. He muttered under his breath, "But she is so pretty, how can that be possible?"

I, too, had a hard time understanding. Why wouldn't he, too? Unfortunately, my father died six months later. I was never able to have the conversation that would have eased his mind.

When I left for Los Angeles, my mom and I hardly said a word to each other. Pam gave me many hugs and told me to stay strong. For three weeks, my mom and I didn't talk. It was so foreign to me. I was used to speaking to my mom at least once a day, every day. Finally, she called and told me she loved me. She said that she didn't understand, but she didn't want to lose me, and she promised to work on it. I was so moved and so happy that her love for me was more important than her fear.

A few months later, my mom came to a big event for MECLA (the Municipal Election Committee of Los Angeles, a political action committee supporting and contributing funds to political candidates in favor of human rights and, in particular, gay rights). It was a formal affair, and oh, how beautiful my mom was! With her hair up in a French roll and her gorgeous gown, she looked like Grace Kelly. She entered the gala on the arms of two handsome young men in tuxes, with all eyes beholding her in awe. It was a wonderful evening—a milestone for us and the beginning of a profound understanding. She had a fabulous time seeing gay men and women, who were happy, authentic, and doing something meaningful for this world.

I share this journey of coming out, so others who might read this book will understand how difficult it is for many of us. I was unable to find my power until I let go of my secret. We are all the same. Everyone has challenges, and everyone suffers from the loneliness we feel when we shut down and suppress our truths. Though the secret of being gay was extremely painful and isolating, it helped me understand others' struggles, making me more empathetic and compassionate. What made me the teacher I am today was giving myself permission to come out. Every week, I do a free mini-class for a group of new students as a way to give back. I out myself each week, hoping this will help others to do the same. This is what has made me find my power—the courage to share my truth.

IT'S NOT DIRT, IT'S SOIL FOR GROWTH

We all think we have "dirt," or a secret that we should hide. Most often, the thing we may feel ashamed of is only a human experience. Burying our secret is like trying to grow a garden in the basement. You must bring the dirt out into the sunlight. After all, it's only soil, and soil is the basis for new growth.

MARGISM: EXPOSE YOUR TRUTH

1. I will practice sharing my secret with someone I trust.
2. When I "out" myself, I create room for intimacy.
3. By releasing my secret, I make room for joy.

4. I will write my secret down. I will rip the paper into pieces. I will throw it all away and let it go forever.

5. I let the sun in, and from the soil, I will grow and bloom.

Once you've done something that you used to think was impossible, what could ever really scare you again?

—Elliot Page, actor and trans activist

Starla Caldwell's Story— "I'm Fine, I'm Fine"

I'm fifty-four years old. I had been taking acting classes at Margie Haber's Studio for seven months before I actually stepped into "The Margie-sphere."

I had arrived in Los Angeles with hopes of recreating myself once more. I studied at the Stella Adler and Lee Strasberg schools, but left more confused about the process than when I began.

From the beginning, Margie's class and teaching style were different. She communicated in a way I could understand. She gave us permission to open up, and many of the students ran with it. They shared their most personal life experiences, many of which were deeply painful. This was something I could *never* do. My classmates were so vulnerable, and with Margie's empathy and guidance, they felt safe to share. I was, of course, in total denial. So, I didn't share. I told everyone that I didn't have any painful stories. If anyone ever asked me how I was, my answer was always, "I'm fine." Margie didn't force me to open up. She waited.

Finally, the weekend was over, and Margie told us that we should continue to create and that we were all invited to join her ongoing classes. So, of course, I accepted her invitation and became an ongoing student.

One day, Margie gave our class a slice involving a married woman who has an affair with another man. The class that day had eight men and one woman . . . me! So I got to do the "slice" eight times, which was helpful, but still I wasn't living the life of the character.

During my private session with Margie that week, she whipped out the same scene for me to work on again. As I zeroed in on the pain, worry, and shame of the character, guess what? I realized this was me. I was this woman. This was my life. I did this to my husband. Overwhelmed with shame, I burst into tears and shared with Margie my story of infidelity. For the first time in my life, I embraced my vulnerability. I shared everything about my life. It was the first time I trusted someone enough to out myself.

Until I was seven years old, I grew up with my older sister, a single Black mother, and my extraordinary, deeply religious grandmother. My grandmother adored my sister and me. She made a safe, loving home for us. I had heard stories of my father, James, but had no connection to him. Then, when I was seven, he resurfaced, and my mom took us with him, away from the only loving home we would ever know. I remember crying and screaming in James's car on the way to Colorado as I watched my grandmother fade in the distance.

In our new home, there was no furniture and no place to feel safe. James's behavior was unpredictable. I never knew what to expect. When James would act out, my mother would pull away out of fear, leaving my sister and me to fend for ourselves. Muted by intimidation, my mom had no voice. If I behaved in a way that disturbed my father, he would beat me with an extension cord. He was so paranoid that if either my sister or I looked at him the wrong way, he would lose control and become unhinged. The only thing we could do was run into the closet and hold each other until the tornado of violence subsided, and we felt safe enough to come out.

I learned that it was best to keep my feelings checked to protect myself. That way of life served me for many years. I got married, had a child, and wore the veil of happiness, but inside, only I knew how much these childhood memories affected my life and my relationships.

After disclosing my childhood and my affair to Margie in our private session, I discovered a new level of freedom to express my true self without shame. It is hard to put into words the relief that I felt and the power that surged through me as I released all these secrets. That day, Margie became my acting life coach. Because I was willing to get out of my comfort zone, I could use all that I had endured in the creative process. After outing myself, a new Starla was born. I didn't need to hide anymore.

ON THE SPECTRUM

An actress, Sue Ann Pien, was up for a new series, playing a character on the autism spectrum. Sue Ann is also on the spectrum. She was uncertain about playing someone so similar to herself. When Sue Ann entered my house for a private session, she was smiling and connecting with me. I wouldn't have guessed that she had Asperger's. We talked first before getting into the script. She looked straight at me, very focused and connected. Nothing about her seemed characteristic of autism.

We talked about the character. They both were waitresses at a diner, and they both had similar behavioral characteristics; however, Sue Ann hid them from the world. In one scene, the character was demoted from taking orders at the counter due to expressing unfiltered comments to a customer. She was sent to the back to make french fries.

When we started to create the character, Sue Ann seemed to shut down, completely distant from the character. I asked her to share with me what she was feeling. I told her that I had worked as a speech therapist in my first career and had taught autistic children.

After a short time, Sue Ann began to trust me and opened up about her secret. When she was a child, her mother tried to cover up that she was different. It was drilled into her to always look at the other person and keep her voice in a natural tone. This served her as an actress who had to hide her truth in order to book parts. This effort, however, required a constant need to control her behavior, which was damaging to her soul. Now that Sue Ann was given an opportunity to live a life that had the same challenges, she was petrified to out herself.

I took her hand and gently shared: "You are a beautiful person. Asperger's doesn't define you. I know how hard it is to be different." After that, Sue Ann jumped into the script with the courage it took to be her authentic self. I gave her permission to merge her life with the characters—to cry, to be angry, to be in her body, and use the behavior that she had hidden all these years.

Afterward, we hugged, and we both felt such love for each other. My son came in as she was leaving, and Sue Ann let go of her controlled behavior. "You are so handsome. I like you. You could be a movie star!" she declared, playfully vocalizing as she closed the door. Michael smiled, too, as he was used to all sorts of actors coming and going in my house.

Sue Ann and I worked together on three callbacks and she booked the lead in this new Amazon series! We continued working together to create the life of her new character. I'm so proud of her.

Derek's Story—
Sports Mentality

My absolute fear was being vulnerable, being judged.

I grew up playing sports. There is a certain idea of masculinity in sports. Don't show emotion. Don't share your feelings. If you're hurt, play through it. Be a "man." Covered with sweat, my lungs burning, I knew the game plan as a player and teammate inside out: practicing the simplest of things over and over and over again, getting instant feedback from my coaches and teammates, and knowing if I were right or wrong, I would either celebrate or get yelled at right then and there. I knew this world. I became a professional soccer player and wore my armor of success without having to share any inner feelings.

But acting was the complete opposite.

There is no safe place. No one is there with you. There isn't even a right or wrong like there is in sports. There's no right path to follow. You also need to have access to other parts of your body, mind, and soul that sports just don't allow you to feel or express. Acting is about sharing the full range of human emotion. But how can you express those emotions if all you'd ever done was hide what you truly felt from those around you in case they viewed you as weak, even hiding those thoughts from yourself? I never allowed them out.

Margie opened my mind. It wasn't her telling me what to do. It was literally her holding my hand in a room with twelve other actors on the first day I met her and saying: "It's okay. Tell us your story." I shared the most personal parts of me. While she was holding my hand, I bravely told the story of my brother, who has a rare, crippling, fatal disease. The whole class put their arms around me as I cracked and couldn't stop crying. Margie's compassion allowed me to be vulnerable without judgment, and it was liberating.

That day, I shattered that wall of protection and allowed strangers to fill up my pain and fear with love and kindness. I know I never would have received all that genuine love if I had not been willing to be seen, really seen, inside the place that terrified me. I realized you could go there and come back with more understanding of who you are. That is power.

Rick Springfield's Story— Mr. D

Rick Springfield, my friend and student, always digs deep into his core and bravely acknowledges his greatest fears. Despite all of his accomplishments—the gold and platinum albums, sold-out concerts, his Grammy Awards and nominations, American Music Awards, a happy family life, and all the money he could need, Rick still experiences apprehensions that could defeat him.

As he writes in his remarkable bestselling memoir, *Late, Late at Night:*

> The darkness is pushing me. There are times when I have awakened in the middle of the night and seen him sitting there on the end of the bed, My Darkness. He whispers to me and fills my head with fears and doubts that I can't shake, that keep me tossing and turning until the sun cracks the morning sky. Now, as I pace around the pool, trying to take desperate inventory of all the awesome shit I've accomplished, my skin is crawling at the terrible awareness of this reality gap between where I appear to be—successful, happy, complete— and where I really am inside my head: no happier than before

I started this journey. Writing has been a saving grace when I'm depressed . . . Mr. D hates it when I am productive, creative, and actually doing something other than giving him my undivided attention. He is only a child, a selfish prick, and not used to being ignored. (from *Late, Late at Night*, by Rick Springfield, Touchstone, 2010)

Studio Focus: **Conversations from the Classroom**
THE "OUTING OURSELVES" EXERCISE

I begin with a trust exercise that is life-changing for many. I lower the lights and ask everyone to close their eyes and take a journey back to their childhood with me. I tell them to take a few deep breaths and imagine going back to their bedroom when they were a child—whatever age comes up and not to worry about what room pops up for them—just go wherever it takes them. I ask them to listen while in that room—any noises, yelling, screaming, crying, music, or laughter. Then I take them to their window, and I ask them to look outside and experience what they see—breathe—and let it drop down, getting out of their heads. Then I encourage them to feel the floor, check out the walls, and find their bed—imagine laying on it. What does it feel like? Is the bed soft? Hard? Feel the comforter. Are their stuffed animals on the bed? Is the pillow soft? What are the colors that jump out at you? Go back to listening—any noise affecting you? Now, in your imagination, walk over to an object. Touch it. Experience it. Breathe. Did someone special give you this object? How do you feel being close to it again? Breathe.

Then I tell them to open their eyes. Inevitably, most are crying and still in the childhood experience. I pick one student and sit in front of him or her, asking the people on either side to physically connect with that person by touch so he or she is not alone. I encourage that person to stay with me, look into my eyes, share the experience, and to trust me that it is safe.

Some have been raped. Some have seen their father die in front of them; some have experienced such loneliness that they tremble. Others remember the wonderful times and cry because the innocence and love are gone—so many tragedies, so many painful experiences.

The wonderful part of this "outing oneself" is that they no longer have to be controlled by those deplorable memories. Once they let the "puss" out, a miraculous thing occurs during this weekend: the courage to be vulnerable creates true intimacy. Only now can the actor truly live another person's life. What is important to remember is that this is only an exercise to connect to your core and your truths. After that, you need to let it go and not let that part of you control your life and your work. If you do, it becomes self-indulgent, and no one wants to see someone leading with the victim.

I encourage my students to bravely out themselves, step out of their comfort zone, and embrace the truth that we are all equal. Everyone has challenges and all of us have hidden skeletons, but they will no longer control us if we share them with others.

Any wound is real.

—William Stafford, poet and pacifist

POWER CHALLENGE

- On a day-to-day level, do you find yourself using humor as armor in your normal interactions? Describe the times you use it at work, with your significant other, and with your family.

- When do you use anger to protect yourself and with whom? Write down three incidents where that occurred.
- Indifference is a go-to for many when they don't want to be vulnerable. Describe three examples of using indifference in your life.
- How have you learned from your culture to protect yourself? Write three different tools you can use to open up and trust.
- Explore, with your writing, a time when you allowed an arrow of meanness from someone else to pierce deeper than your skin. Describe the feelings you experienced as you went down that road of oversensitivity. Then breathe and write down three times, "It was just a pinch of the skin."
- If you were able to share a secret that's been locked inside of you for years, would it make you feel better? Identify someone in your life you trust. Consider reaching out to them. Practice by writing down the conversation you would want to have with that person.
- What are you protecting underneath your armor? Please take time to look deep within and write down which of these core feelings you are protecting—sadness, pain, fear, love?
- Now, you are ready to list the ways you have learned to remove your armor.

5

Pieces of Ourselves– The Five Ego States

I became an acting coach because I find human beings to be fascinating. We are multilayered like onions. We can keep peeling until we find the center. We often rely on one layer of ourselves, a piece that we have used our whole life, out of fear of revealing more. It is the willingness to go to a deeper layer that can bring true happiness.

One of the ways to be a better communicator and a healthier human being is to understand our different alter egos. Dr. Eric Berne's book *Transactional Analysis in Psychotherapy* divided this phenomenon into three ego states—Parent, Child, and Adult. My brilliant friend, Elaine Harris, who was a therapist, taught me that there are actually five ego states: Critical Parent, Nurturing Parent, Fearful Child, Playful Child, and Adult.

- **Critical Parent:** the voice of disapproval
- **Nurturing Parent:** the voice of compassionate support
- **Fearful Child:** the voice of fear and wanting to hide
- **Playful Child:** the voice of daring to say "fuck it!" and jumping in with both feet

- **Adult:** the voice of reason and competency

Some of these ego states (voices) can take up too much space in our complex minds and be destructive. Other voices fill our mind with joy and tranquility. The goal is to identify each one, accept and befriend each one, and learn to shift with ease into the voice that will best serve you in each circumstance.

* Critical Parent *

Our Critical Parent is the voice that has haunted many of us since we were children. It makes us feel less than.

It is reinforced in our culture in various ways:

"If I'm not the best at everything, then I'll be left behind in life."

"Only becoming a doctor or a lawyer is worthwhile."

"I have to be thin and beautiful to succeed in any business."

"I'm the ugly one in my family. No wonder I don't have a boyfriend."

Many of us need approval, because we didn't get enough love when we were young. Some of us were never hugged or shown any affection. Many actors go into the acting profession because they were never taught to be intimate and need to "live other lives" to get what all people deserve—healthy relationships.

The Critical Parent can rear its ugly head at any time, especially when we least expect it. Just looking in the mirror can bring out this critical voice.

Every day we have reasons to criticize ourselves, "I have to do a presentation to people who are so much smarter than me. They all went to Yale, and I went to Stony Brook." "Oh no, I can't believe she is here auditioning for the same part. I might as well go home now."

The Critical Parent can also be heard when you are hanging around people who don't respect you. All of a sudden, you lose your power, feel small, and accept a meager role in your own existence.

Now, you are back playing an extra in your life. Has that ever happened to you?

We pick ourselves apart ceaselessly and never see the hidden immensity.

—Curtis Tyrone Jones, author and motivational speaker

Terrell Battle's Story— The Sneaky Critical Parent

Finding my power was unique in the fact that I've always had a high level of confidence in the stand-up comedy world. But television acting was a different hill to conquer. On stage, expressing my thoughts, words, and emotions was simple. I've always been this person; being true to myself is the only option as a comedian.

When I'm given a script, I have to become the character on the page, with only elements of my personality infused.

I was cast on the CBS sitcom, *Superior Donuts*, with Emmy Award–winning actor Judd Hirsch, as well as Katey Sagal, David Koechner, and so on. Pretty intimidating cast for a kid who's only done stand-up, a few plays in college, and sketch work.

Season one of the show, I'm doing a scene with Judd. There's an acting coach on set, and I'm reading with her. I'm going over the script in my head. Every waking moment, I'm trying to learn the lines and my character. Every waking moment, I'm trying to not be the one who fucks up.

After running the scene a few times, by now overprepared, I'm on my break and Judd comes over to me and goes, "Hey, kid, you do stand-up, right? Stick to that."

It was a punch to the face. Here I was busting my ass to get this right, and Judd shits on it. I wasn't mad at Judd. I was disappointed in myself. What was I doing wrong? Do I belong here? They might as well have changed my character's name to "Self Doubt."

Later, Judd walks by me and gradually says, "You're already funny. Fuck it."

At that moment, I realized Judd wasn't insulting me. He was telling me to stop trying so hard. You're already funny, and they hired you for a reason, so just throw away the script already.

My Critical Parent had taken over when I was stressing myself out over the lines. I lost and found my power in a span of a few hours. I'm aware that, as artists, we may deal with it time and time again. But next time, I'll be a little more aware of my personal power because of the wisdom of a great actor from *Taxi*.

If babies held the same tendency
toward self-criticism as adults,
they might never learn to walk or talk.

—Dan Millman, author, *Way of the Peaceful Warrior*

* Nurturing Parent *

I was brought up with lots of love and taught to believe that I could do anything, so when my Critical Parent spirals out of control, I have a Nurturing Parent who can step forward.

"I deserve to be loved. I deserve a healthy relationship. I deserve to be successful. I deserve to be financially secure."

I never understood the benefits of the Nurturing Parent until much later in my life. It's often the least utilized of the voices, and yet it's a very powerful one. Nurturing others is easy for most, but nurturing myself? Aye, there's the rub! I have to live for the rest of my life with myself, which makes me the most valued person I know. So, I need to treat myself better.

The Nurturing Parent helps us to be compassionate and forgiving with ourselves and with others.

Sometimes, when I go into a room filled with judgmental people, I turn up the voice of my Nurturing Parent. It gives me lots of hugs and lets me know that we all have insecurities.

Actors, especially, need this voice when they go into the casting director's office. It's not easy to walk into a room of various executives, camera people, and others deeply involved with the production. Usually, someone's on the phone, others might be eating, and the casting director may not give you the time of day. This is when your Nurturing Parent can step in to help you.

"Darling, you're going to be fine. You are going to flourish in this moment. These are good people. They are just stressed out. They have this one project, and everyone in this room is scared that they are not going to find the right person for the role, so their jobs are on the line."

You can call forward your Nurturing Parent at a party where you feel you don't fit in. Let yourself hear the Nurturing Parent voice: "Anyone at this party would be lucky to get to know you. Darling, you are a beautiful person!"

Makes you feel powerful, eh?

If you can show people how to build castles, make sure you do not neglect building and nurturing your own.

—Suzy Kassem, writer, poet, and philosopher

Madalyn Horcher's Story—
I Love Me!

Margie had asked the class, "How can you expect to live the life of a character if you don't even know who you are?" Pretty simple question, but it scared me to my very core because, at the time, I was going through a period in my life where I had no sense of identity. I remember going home, lying in my bed, and crying for a good three hours because I realized that I was clueless! I had no idea who I was, and even worse, I was my own worst enemy when it came to the thing I love most in my life, acting.

Over the course of a couple of weeks, I beat myself up over Margie's magic question, trying to pinpoint how I got to this place. I crumbled under the weight of my Critical Parent and my Fearful Child, "Of course it won't work out for you. You're not good enough! You are too weak, too stupid, and not pretty enough. Why do you bother?"

Then my Fearful Child would scream at me when it came to a relationship, "You shouldn't let that person go. What if you never find someone who loves you again? OMG, I'll never be with anyone!"

But something amazing happened. When those voices took over, my Nurturing Parent swooped in and responded with "Hey, you beautiful soul. It's gonna be okay! You are so special and so strong! Don't worry about anyone else's timeline. It'll happen for you, you talented person! You will meet the right one who will make you happy. You don't have to settle."

By giving power to the Nurturing voice in my head, it helped me understand that I have the right to forgive myself for my mistakes and that it's okay to be . . . human. Knowing thyself is a journey and an acceptance that we all deserve and have a right to experience.

Don't brood. Get on with living
and loving. You don't have forever.

—Leo Buscaglia, author and motivational speaker

MARGISM: FALL IN LOVE ... WITH YOU

Every time I pass a mirror, I will look at myself and say, "I love you."
I will shower myself with compassion and forgiveness.
I will list the things I love about myself.
I am my own Valentine.

☀ Fearful Child ☀

Oh, how the Fearful Child voice takes over at unexpected times! The Fearful Child is crafty. It can prevent us from taking chances and exploring a relationship.

The Fearful Child comes to the surface in many situations:

"I am going to cancel my job interview and stay in bed."

"They have to tell me what to do because I'm too afraid I'll make the wrong decision."

"I dropped a line in my scene. I want to run away. Get me out of here."

You lose your life by getting smaller and smaller and physically stepping back in hopes that no one will notice you. It is the voice that plunges us into the terrible state of doubt. It conspires with the Critical Parent to make us feel powerless.

I have experienced this voice throughout my life. It was loudest when I adopted my son just after he was born:

I am so scared.

What if I drop him?

He is so tiny.

He's going to fall off the jungle gym if he doesn't come down.

I am so scared that I am not going to be a good enough parent.

When Michael started driving, I was the worst kind of helicopter parent:

Text me when you leave.

Text me when you get there.

Text me when you get home!

The plane's going down, and I will never see him again! (I get very dramatic.)

Does your Fearful Child get out of control at times like mine?

Therapy Session—Stop Avoiding! Face My Fear!

MARGIE

Just when I think I am the Adult . . . *bang!* I fall deeply into a pit of fear.

THERAPIST

Face your fear. Escape is not a choice. Face who and what you are afraid of—risk being rejected.

MARGIE

My avoidance is part of my Fearful Child. When I am scared to look at myself, I use distractions—watching television, working, and keeping busy. I believe I will be okay if I just keep moving. But, during those times, I'm not willing to jump out of that ego.

THERAPIST

Avoidance is the lie, the illusion, and the fantasy. But there was something more important. You said, "I wasn't willing."

MARGIE

Right.

THERAPIST

That's more conscious.

MARGIE

I'm leading with my Fearful Child. I especially get stuck there when I am in preference. When my wife Susan and I argue, I am afraid that she will hurt me emotionally. I am vulnerable.

THERAPIST

It's your relationship to your fear.

MARGIE

I love Susan and kiss and hug her, but I'm waiting for the other shoe to drop. When she gets anxious, I allow it to trigger me: "Oh, here we go again. Now, it's going to happen." And then, like a clam, I shut down. My Fearful Child puts me in the "preference" mode. I prefer that she would be open and loving, and I'm stuck in that preference.

THERAPIST

I'd also prefer it if someone peeled my grapes, and, you know, blah, blah, blah.

MARGIE

Oh God, yes. I haven't learned my lesson yet.

THERAPIST

And what is that lesson?

MARGIE

I can bring out my Nurturing Parent to take care of my Fearful Child, leaving room for me to choose to be empathetic and say, "That's what Susan's going through, and it has nothing to do with me."

THERAPIST

When you say you have a choice, I'm going to say that's dicey. I'm not going to give you a choice of being compassionate, loving, forgiving, kind, or warm.

MARGIE

When I am afraid of getting hurt, it takes a lot of practice to let go of leading with that Fearful Child so that I can be there for others.

THERAPIST

We all have to build that muscle. Give love to yourself first. Loving is a gift. Warmness is a gift, compassion is a gift, forgiving is a gift, and service is a gift. You're on the right road.

DOUBT IS OUR ENEMY

Fear is defined as a distressing emotion aroused by impending danger, evil, pain, and so on, whether the feeling is real or imagined. Being afraid of dying, being sick, or having something catastrophic occur all get labeled as fear.

What many of us don't realize is that doubt is totally based on the fear that feeds the Fearful Child. Doubt is so cunning that we don't always recognize it.

We all have the tendency to believe in self-doubt and self-criticism, but listening to this voice never gets us closer to our goals. Instead, try from the point of view of a mentor or good friend who believes in you, wants the best for you, and will encourage you when you feel discouraged.

—Kelly McGonigal, health psychologist and lecturer, Stanford Universtiy

Brandon Scott is a student of mine. During the time I have been working with him, he's been in four series: *Dead to Me, 13 Reasons*

Why, This Is Us, and most recently, *Goliath.* He is doing rather well! And yet, even with all the success he has had, the Fearful Child brings doubt to his life—"Am I actually good? Am I fooling everyone?"

Brandon Scott's Story— From Rehearsal to Shooting *Goliath*

I booked the series *Goliath* and was pretty stoked. I had been working with Margie on different slices and thought I was ready for the rehearsal. But then doubt crept in when I realized we were going to rehearse a slice that we had not created. I didn't want to do it. When I got to the rehearsal, I was excited to see whom they cast. I was thinking, If they only knew how I felt about this slice.

As we prepared to rehearse, another actor sat down with me and said, "I'm so nervous. Are you?" I couldn't get over how he immediately admitted to his fear. That kind of broke the ice and made me let go of my nerves.

I made an appointment with Margie to go over that slice. My message to her was, "I hate this slice."

Her response was, "You don't hate it. You are scared of it. It's easier to hate the slice than to look at your truth."

When we sat down to create it, I realized that Margie was correct. It was my fear that elicited that response. I didn't understand the complexity of my character and therefore judged the slice. I also didn't think I was going to be good in it. It was easier to hate the slice than to face my fear. Once we created it, I loved it! It was a good lesson that, if I immediately say I don't like something and don't want to do it, maybe I should take a moment and see what is happening on the inside. Margie also reminded me that, when I doubt myself, I should start listening to the Nurturing Parent and the Playful Child. "You are very talented. You deserve to be suc- *— Positive Affirm* cessful. You are worthy. Enjoy it!"

Then came the actual shoot. I was ready. I had made my choices, memorized my lines, and knew everything about my character. But I was thrown a curve when I was encouraged to let go and do whatever inspires me. They were cool with the lines changing. They trusted me to live outside of the box that I had crammed my character into as preparation. They gave me all this freedom that I always wanted, but I didn't know what to do with it.

My Fearful Child was wreaking havoc as I was given permission to be creative. I thought, Um, what if my being in the moment isn't right? I remember when I first started in this business. I loved doing theater because I had so many opportunities to stretch my character. I complained that I couldn't do the same thing in television and film because that process was always about not taking up too much time. And here I was, being given the opportunity to do a creative show that keeps evolving and keeps me on my toes, and I was frightened. The Fearful Child was giving me erroneous advice, saying, "You have to get this right." And the Critical Parent was saying that if I don't, then I am not good enough. So, I had to lower those voices and replace them with the Nurturing Parent, the Adult, and the Playful Child. All three voices are important to me.

The Adult can state the specific reasons why I should not listen to the Fearful Child and the Critical Parent. "You were chosen for this part because you know what you are doing. You are very good at improvisation, and you have created this character specifically with Margie. You can do anything if you make up your mind to do so." Then my underused Nurturing Parent, in a loving tone, supported me. "Hey, little Boss (my nickname), I am so proud of you. You are so talented. You are going to be terrific!" And last, my Playful Child humorously shouts, "Fuck it! Let's play!"

Sometimes it is hard for me to hear the supportive, loving Nurturing Parent. Maybe if I can raise that voice, it will help me to get to my Playful Child quicker. There are times I feel like I am doing a Hail Mary pass. It's like I get pushed to that point where I have nothing left to lose, so the Fearful Child actually helps me to say, "What the hell?" The problem is I don't necessarily get there in a kind way. Maybe the Nurturing Parent can help me with that. Even when I finished shooting, I got in bed and analyzed it through the lens of the Critical Parent. I felt like, if I hadn't done that, I could have enjoyed the experience more. Is it too much freedom? Brandon ten years ago was all about freedom and enjoying the process. Now that I am successful, a series regular, where is the fun? I have to trust my creativity. Be kind to myself. And remember why I did this acting in the first place. Go create and enjoy!

Remember, the Fearful Child doesn't go away. It's always there. So, be kind to it. We want to push it away, but you need to listen to the voice of the Fearful Child and validate it, nurture it.

I will now say to my Fearful Child: "Excuse me. Do you need some attention? I am going to give you a little space that is all your own, and I will take care of you." You are most powerful when you know that no one, not even your Fearful Child, can take your creativity away from you.

> *Of all the liars in the world, sometimes*
> *the worst are our own fears.*

—Rudyard Kipling, author

> *We nurture our creativity when we release*
> *our inner child. Let it run and roam free. It*
> *will take you on a brighter journey.*

—Serina Hartwell, author

* Playful Child *

The Playful Child voice sets us free. It can burst forth with those two magic words, *fuck it!*

The Playful Child sparks our creativity without being afraid that there will be consequences.

Who cares what anyone else thinks? I'm jumping out of this box!
I'm going to laugh and enjoy being me.
I'm ready to give it all a go.

Tragically, the Playful Child is squeezed out of us by the Adult rules of "correct" behavior. I refuse to play by those rules. I have always had a big Playful Child energy and always preferred to take risks rather than be stuck in my comfort zone.

I loved life from the get-go and never wanted to sacrifice my Playful Child. I would sing loudly walking home from school, even when others stared. Sometimes, however, my Fearful Child is disguised as my Playful Child. When I am not centered or feel insecure, I tend to scatter my energy to every corner of the room instead of being present with whomever or whatever is right in front of me at that moment. It is difficult but, after all, I am a work in progress.

A BIG *MACHER*

My rabbi asked if I would work with a very prominent, recently elected politician from Israel. (I can't reveal the name, but he was a big *macher*, which is Yiddish for "big shot.")

A rather distinguished, middle-aged man in a dark gray suit with a white, button-down shirt stepped out of a luxurious limousine onto my driveway. A familiar greeting, shalom (the Hebrew word for "peace"), was expressed by both of us as he kissed the mezuzah by my front door and entered.

His predecessor had been an exceptional public speaker, but it was not his forte. He wanted me to give him tips he could quickly write down to accomplish this challenge. I respectfully declined as I explained tips would not do the trick. He said that he was scheduled to go back to Israel and give a speech to thirty-five thousand people.

"Well," I announced, "we better get started."

I asked him to get up and give me an example of his speech. Hmm, how can I describe it? Though he spoke excellent English, I didn't understand one thing he was saying! It was filled with statistics and data that could have easily been given as a handout to his audience. His Adult was on full throttle, and the Playful Child was nowhere to be found. Though he was a nice man, I explained that if he didn't enjoy what he was saying, the audience wouldn't either. So, I took him through an exercise I use with clients who need to bring out their Playful Child. I asked him to describe a random picture. Then, I asked him to imagine he was describing this picture to an eight-year-old child and to use as many adjectives as possible. Here's how it went:

"There is this huge, pink elephant in the middle of the ocean sitting on a large purple shark. On top of the elephant is a bicycle with a pyramid of five clowns wearing masks attached to long snorkels piercing out of the water."

"That is the silliest thing I have ever said." He laughed, unable to keep a straight face. I said, "Yes. And it did the trick. Your Playful Child has arisen!"

His favorite group from the sixties was the Beatles, so I had him move around to "I Want to Hold Your Hand" to help him find the Playful Child in his body. Then we were ready to tackle his speech. We took out most of the statistics and data, which would be passed out at the event, and brought in his humanity. We came up with a humorous story to begin and sprinkled this conversation (I always remove the word "speech") with vulnerability. This "one hour to give me some tools" lesson became three hours of pure joy. Finally, he left, humming "Eleanor Rigby" and thanking me for giving him permission to have fun.

Studio Focus: Conversations from the Classroom
I'M A ROLLER-COASTER FANATIC!

INT. CLASSROOM—DAY

MARGIE

I use the Playful Child in my life to free me, to find my own power. I'd love to have a conversation about your Playful Child and the role it plays in your life.

LISA

At twenty-four years old, I had already realized how "unplayful" I was. I thought, *Wow, I'm such a frigging adult.* I was succeeding in theater, but the competitiveness killed all the joy. As a mom, I found it again. Oh, I'm with little playful children all the time. And that was wonderful. But in my career, in my work, did I allow that? Did I see being playful as a valuable trait? No. I thought: *Oh, I've got to be serious. I've got to get the job.* What I've learned in this training session with you, Margie, is that my Playful Child can be an asset.

And so, I am here to acknowledge that I'm enough. I now honor this part of me as an important tool to living that life and freeing myself up to create. The permission has been life-changing, just amazing.

MARGIE

Lisa, you've changed so much. Your Playful Child is free now. Your life is filled with joy. Tell me about your Playful Child, Jackson, and how you experience it as an eighteen-year-old?

JACKSON

In my life, I'm full of the Playful Child. But then it's really strange how, when I approach acting, I feel like I have to drop it. The first step is acknowledging, "Yeah, you're allowed to do this. That's what you need to bring to the table."

BRYCE

Growing up, I received a lot of negative feedback about my Playful Child. Consequently, I hid my Playful Child, and I've struggled to find it again.

MARGIE

I love when you trust your Playful Child, Bryce. Your face lights up. Sally, you have a contagious Playful Child.

SALLY

I have a very natural Playful Child, and it brings me such great joy. I want to make people happy. I want people to feel good in my presence. But I have a very sensitive button with it, so if someone tells me, "Oh, be quiet, you're too loud." It triggers something inside me. I don't remember my personality being squashed as a child. But I will shut down very quickly because it is a vulnerable thing, isn't it? You have to be so open.

MARGIE

Yes. People don't get that the Playful Child is vulnerable. There are those of you in this room with a strong Fearful Child or a strong Critical Parent. How have you used the Playful Child to help you? Good morning, Brooke. How is the Playful Child helping you in your life?

BROOKE

I guess just connecting with a sense of fun. As soon as you said that, I was like, "Oh, I don't have much to comment on. I'm afraid to bring out my Playful Child. If I expose joy and love and it gets shut down, I will go backward."

MARGIE

We are all a work in progress. It's great that you are aware you are inhibiting your Playful Child. Keep reminding yourself, "Wait, that voice is the voice I want to support. Bring it on. It's not loud enough!" Daniel, where in your life could you use more Playful Child? And how can you amplify that voice?

DANIEL

I can use more of the Playful Child in every aspect of my life. Yesterday, I went to Kings Island with my cousin, which is an amusement park. I'm a roller coaster fanatic. When the roller coaster started, I just threw my hands in the air and screamed and just had so much fun. I thought, *If only all of life could be like this.*

MARGIE

Maybe not all of life, but a great percentage could be playful and carefree. The Critical Parent may say, "Stop it. You're an idiot." Fearful Child is, "Oh, I'm so afraid that people are going to judge me." But the Playful Child says, "Fuck it. I want to ride that roller coaster." Let's all go with Daniel on that Roller Coaster and reach our arms straight up as we free fall through the sky!

> *People rarely succeed unless they have fun in what they are doing.*

—Dale Carnegie, author,
How to Win Friends and Influence People

⁎ Adult ⁎

We need our Adult voice. It helps us make important decisions. You need to get an education, be responsible and pay your bills. It is the voice that gets you to your appointments on time. It is the voice of reason. And you need it to survive in this chaotic world. However, it can be tricky. The Adult can be an impediment in some situations. As an acting coach, I observe my students, going over every line to make sure they know exactly what is going on in the script. They take notes constantly. They memorize their lines. They work on their scenes for hours, hoping to get it right. All of this keeps them locked in their technical mind rather than their creative mind. The Adult voice that says, "Be perfect, get an A," does not serve them. My corporate clients believe the most legitimate part of their personality is their Adult, sacrificing creative new ideas that come with playfulness.

All of these voices are essential components of the human psyche.

Studio Focus: Conversations from the Classroom
DO I REALLY NEED THAT EXTRA GLASS OF WINE?

INT. CLASSROOM—DAY

MARGIE
How do we use the Adult in a positive way?

JACKSON
All of us sitting here right now are proof that our Adult is coming through loud and clear.

MARGIE
That's true because everyone's on Zoom now. The Adult is saying, "This is what is good for me." The Adult, in negative terms, tries to be in control and closes off the Playful Child. Jack, is your Adult strong?

JACK
My Adult is strong now.

MARGIE
You say now; what was it before?

JACK
Before, I was always doing what people told me I should do to get where I wanted to go. I left decisions to a parent or a casting director. I felt ashamed about it. Now, I'm doing what I want to do as the Adult.

MARGIE
You can't control everything, but your Adult is a good voice to listen to for advice.

JACK

Totally.

MARGIE

I always say structure is your friend, because structure is an Adult reaction. Control is not an Adult. Control is the Critical Parent and the Fearful Child.

JACK

I totally agree. Structure makes me feel powerful.

MARGIE

Do you need structure to manage your life better? I need it. My son needs it. He gets up in the morning. He does his yoga, workout, and then music. Structure is an Adult ego state.

KEELIA

I have been disguising my Adult for a long time with my Critical Parent and my Fearful Child. When I lost my dad about eight years ago, I had just graduated from college. I did not understand how to create a structure for myself when I was in this fragile, emotional place. I was lost. My Adult was nowhere to be found. Now, five years later, I'm in the most beneficial part of my Adult self because I have a routine. I even stop after two glasses of wine so I can be sharp when I wake up in the morning and do yoga.

SARAH

I'm strongly driven by the Adult versus the other voices within my brain. And that's from being a mom. I was a mom really young. I needed to be an adult. I had to have structure, or I would have spiraled downward. It can be a crutch. "Follow the plan. Follow the plan." I've struggled to voice my Playful Child. I like to pretend I'm spontaneous, but I'm not really.

MARGIE

Spontaneity is important to let us play. I'll end by saying this: The Adult can serve you really well. But we confuse it with other voices. We confuse it with the Critical Parent all the time. If that voice puts you down, that's not the Adult. The Adult is neutral and knows what's best for you. The Adult is the voice that guides us to be our healthiest selves.

MARGISM: INVITE YOUR ADULT IN

When I befriend the Critical Parent and Fearful Child and accept them, the Adult gives me the insight to proceed:

I don't have to explain or complain.

I am aware of where the other person ends and where I begin.

I take a breath before I react or respond to negative texts.

I don't have to win. I can allow that the other person may be right.

I don't have to be a know-it-all.

I can approach every interaction with "easy does it."

Adults tend to repress their pleasure. Sad to say, I think we become adults only through disappointment, grief, and lies.

—Jean-Louis Gassée, business executive

∗ Know Thyself ∗

If we take the time to examine ourselves, we can see which of the five ego states are being supportive and which are screaming for attention. Melina gives us an example of using the three ways to know thyself (Acknowledge. Be Proactive. And Accept.)

Melina Bartzokis's Story— My Five Voices

Critical Parent

Acknowledge	My Critical Parent comes up at work. I get defensive when I mess up. I feel like I am being scolded by my teacher. I feel stupid.
Be Proactive	I separate from my Critical Parent by validating how smart I am.
Accept	It takes time to forgive myself.

Nurturing Parent

Acknowledge	I acknowledge that my Nurturing Parent is underutilized.
Be Proactive	I engage in conversations. "Listen, darling. I am always by your side, helping you to be kind to yourself."
Accept	Be patient. I'm not always going to access it easily.

Fearful Child

Acknowledge	My Fearful Child acts out when I argue with my mom and sister. They are all I have.
Be Proactive	I breathe and call forth my Nurturing Parent as well as seek help from my boyfriend and friends.
Accept	I accept my Fearful Child but give it a small place to live inside of me.

Playful Child

Acknowledge	I am mostly a Playful Child and an Adult with my boyfriend. I acknowledge the importance of my humor that keeps us in balance.

| Be Proactive | My boyfriend and I do this thing where we crawl into each other's arms and say, playfully, "I'm da baby" when we need love and attention. |
| Accept | I'm lucky to have someone to play with lovingly. I accept our problems because, with Drew, no forgiving is necessary because we deal with them quickly. |

Adult

Acknowledge	I have a very strong Adult voice, but it can get in my way when I use it to create.
Be Proactive	When need be, I will relinquish the Adult to the Playful Child.
Accept	I have a wonderful Adult as well. I am a work in progress.

Ignorance is the parent of fear.

—*Moby-Dick* by Herman Melville

Studio Focus: **Conversations from the Classroom**
YOU'RE ENOUGH THE DAY YOU WERE BORN

INT. CLASSROOM—DAY

ADAM

I have been auditioning a lot and going through a breakup. Margie, I remember you talking about giving your power away to someone else and wanting to be validated by another. I had an epiphany that all of the five voices exist simultaneously in real time. It's a matter of deciding which one to listen to. All actors have a need for some degree of validation that comes from difficulties in our childhood. We wrestle with it. I realize that I still have a part of me that wants to show my dad that I am good at something. It doesn't drive me. I don't wake up and say, "Today, I'm going to prove it to him," but I do have this deeper desire to have myself be seen, and I am afraid it's not going to happen. I guess that's my Fearful Child.

RICHARD

Is that through your eyes or through your dad's eyes?

ADAM

Well, it's through mine. But I am beginning to understand that his validation isn't my road to happiness. What I am tinkering with is that my dad does love me, and I am enough, and it wouldn't matter. So, I now say from my Nurturing Parent voice, "You are always enough, Adam, from the day you were born."

MARGIE

There are so many of us who just want to be seen and loved by our parents or significant other. We are afraid of being unworthy and are always looking for validation from another rather than from within. It is universal, isn't it?

DAKOTA

I have a very loud survival brain, which is my Adult, which limits me from getting out of my comfort zone. Survival doesn't mean thriving. It means surviving at the bare minimum. So, there are always going to be things that come up.

MARGIE

So, let's use this as a piece of the five voices. How would you use the voices in that scenario?

DAKOTA

My Critical Parent is saying, "If you are not going to be prepared or working at your best, then you will fall through the cracks. You are not going to make it."

MARGIE

So, it's the fear of failure.

DAKOTA

Yes, and fear of not being good enough.

MARGIE

What do the other voices say to you?

DAKOTA

I hear my Adult say, "When you are learning something new, you are fine-tuning your craft. It's a good thing."

MARGIE

And the Nurturing Parent? Please say it in the tone of that voice.

DAKOTA

"It's okay. I love you. Everything changes."

MARGIE

And the Playful Child?

MARGIE AND DAKOTA

"Let's have some fun, baby, let's have some fun!"

The class laughs.

Laughter is poison to fear.

—George R.R. Martin, author, *A Song of Ice and Fire*

Conversation with Fiona Goodwin, Psychotherapist

FIONA

You grew up with a distorted image of what you thought life would be like and what life would bring you.

MARGIE

Yes, when I was a child, I could do no wrong. My dad would say, "Do Ed Sullivan for me," and I always got rewards. They looked at me as an adorable person.

FIONA

Hmm, that seems so weird. (We both laugh.) I can't relate to it.

MARGIE

Everyone thought I should be so healthy with such a loving family. But I also hid being gay from a very young age. That was a scar.

   I found out later that life isn't this Disneyland that I grew up in. It means my inner child is often bruised and prone to tantrums at times.

FIONA

The way that I would work with that is to have a dialogue with your Nurturing Parent and your Fearful Child, who could be quite enraged, hurt, and disappointed.

MARGIE

Why wasn't I more prepared? Why didn't my parents teach me that the world couldn't be seen through a rose-colored lens?

FIONA

Well, thankfully, you didn't grow up in a perfect environment, otherwise, you would be unbearably happy! (Laughter) And you wouldn't have any friends!

MARGIE

True. (More laughter)

FIONA

In working with yourself, we would allow your Fearful Child to have a voice, and your Nurturing Parent would invite your Fearful Child to talk to her. "Please, I need to understand you.

We need to work together and be in a relationship together to form a powerful team."

MARGIE

What you are saying is that the Nurturing Parent is encouraging the Fearful Child to speak up and express her feelings of anger, sadness, and fear. But what is the Adult's part?

FIONA

The difference is the Adult says: "I need you to educate me. I need you to tell me what is going on."

MARGIE

But what if the Critical Parent kicks in and says: "What is wrong with you? You had such a perfect life."

FIONA

You need to let the Critical Parent express herself.

MARGIE

Really? Are you sure? I have always quashed it. I have been afraid of my shame.

FIONA

Exactly. However, the Nurturing Parent might say at some point, "Sweetheart, you are far too kind to talk to your child in such a hurtful way." Then the Adult can join the conversation. "It is advantageous to allow the Critical Parent to be heard."

MARGIE

Ah hah. That is so helpful. I used to think of the Adult coming from empathy, but actually, it's detached.

FIONA

Yes, the Adult is like a manager, an intermediary—someone who sees the whole picture. The Adult values every voice.

MARGIE

Yes, very good. Don't put down your Critical Parent. It can serve you.

FIONA

Yes, all five ego states serve a vital function in the eternal quest of becoming a healthy human being.

Avoiding danger is no safer in the long run than outright exposure. The fearful are caught as often as the bold.

—Helen Keller, author and disability rights activist

* Go-Tos Burn Through My Self-Esteem *

We each like to think we have our MO (modus operandi, or method of operation), but often we respond to life from our go-to. For some, it might be a Fearful Child go-to, others involuntarily fall into a Critical Parent response as a go-to.

Does your go-to serve you? Does it help you become the lead in your own life?

Right. I thought so. Me neither.

Your go-tos are bad habits. They don't allow you to be present because they stop you from being affected by the person in front of you.

As soon as my Critical Parent hijacks my brain, I already assume I know the direction the conversation is going.

One afternoon, we, the longtime "girls in the 'hood" friends, did a Zoom call to catch up. One of my friends said, "Let's go around the squares and see how everyone is."

My Critical Parent had already decided that I was going to be forgotten, so, of course, that happened. My fear of being invisible brought out the Fearful Child and Critical Parent. The script in my head was: *Are they going to skip me? Of course, they left me out. They think I talk too much.*

My self-esteem was burned up by my go-to responses.

Then (thank God for therapy) it occurred to me that I had choices.

I can go-to a different piece of me. I chose my Nurturing Parent. *Affirmation* "They love you. You must love yourself. You are worthy, and what you have to offer is golden."

If your go-to is the Fearful Child or the Critical Parent, you need to shift to the healthy voices through trust. Trust yourself. Trust the other parts of you that make you feel powerful. If I trust myself, then I can trust others.

> You have been criticizing yourself for years
> and it hasn't worked. Try approving of
> yourself and see what happens.

—Louise Hay, author and founder of Hay House

Nikko Austen Smith's Story— I'm Too White

I definitely have a go-to that does not serve me. Growing up as a Black girl, I was always told that I speak, dress, and act too white. As if white is its own personality. I was made fun of by those in my own community who looked just like me. When I was twenty-one, something changed in me. I wanted to connect more with my community. I wanted to be a strong Black woman that the media was telling me I should be. I began to read tons of books about my history (Malcolm X, Assata Shakur, the Black Panther Movement, Jimmy Hendrix, etc.). I adopted a hardened nature and began to hold my head up higher, began to see things more clearly, began to understand who I was, where I came from, and how proud my ancestors would be of me for finally figuring it all out. Little did I know, I had nothing figured out. It was all a facade.

This, of course, transferred over to my work as an actor. I wanted to scream at everyone, through my work, that I was intelligent, strong, and *Black*. No one could ever say that I act, speak, or carry myself in a white manner. I was angry at the world, and that anger came through as my crutch, my go-to. I used it to fuel the strength in my voice and the weight in my steps. It helped me to land a role on a show focused on Black culture! I assumed if it worked once, it would work for everything else. Then I became stuck.

I find my voices chime in on my life a lot, especially when I am in an awkward situation and a person, usually not of color, says a remark that is, quite honestly, offensive and racist. My Critical Parent would, and still often does, creep in and tell me, "You're not Black enough, Nikko. You don't know enough about your history or politics to tell them they are wrong. Who are you? You're a fraud." My Fearful Child would squirm, saying, "What are people going to think of me? I'm so scared that I'm going to be seen as a fraud. How could you even think to speak up for yourself? People are going to think you're crazy. They are going to call you the angry Black woman behind your back." I can learn to use my Playful Child to say, "Fuck it, Nikko! You barely know this bitch! Tell them it upsets you. It's not gonna hurt! C'mon!!"

I need to learn to listen to my Nurturing Parent, who would say something like, "Nikko, you are a wonderful person. You know who you are, where you come from, and where you're going. You're very smart. You know you can speak up for whatever is on your mind. I'm proud of you." I can learn to listen to my Adult, who would say, "You can either suck it up this one time, and if it persists, then talk to those people about their comments, or you can speak to them privately in a calm manner and tell them how their comments affected you and why. No angry Black woman here."

I'm aware of when the Fearful Child and Critical Parent appear in my ear. Usually, it occurs when I'm in the sticky situation of, "Should I or should I not educate this person?" Or when I'm about to go in for a major audition. Or when I speak amongst those in my community who are truly all and for the people, those who know all the facts, all the history. The feelings I put on myself are the feelings of "unwelcomeness," because I know deep down that I am not heavily versed in the works of Jean-Michel Basquiat, Mary McLeod Bethune, or Toni Morrison. I feel, for lack of better words, stupid. That's what those voices tell me. I can take action by telling myself that I know what I know. There were many influential Black activists, doctors, writers, musicians, singers, inventors . . . the list goes on and on. If I want to know all of them, I'll have to truly study, and that's okay. There are tons of people of different ethnicities who do not know every influential person of that particular ethnicity. It's okay, sis. I forgive myself. I forgive myself. I forgive myself.

It's okay, Nikko. You know yourself.

> There are times when fear is good.
> It must keep its watchful place
> at the heart's controls.

—Aeschylus, playwright, poet, and author, *The Oresteia: Agamemnon, The Libation Bearers, The Eumenides*

Don't be afraid to try something. It never hurts as bad as you think to fail. You seldom regret what you do. You regret what you didn't do. Don't try to be invulnerable. Don't worry too much about security. If you build a wall around yourself, you become a prisoner of that wall. Take a chance.

—Hugh Downs, NBC anchor and host on his retirement

* Creating from Home (Pandemic 2020–2021) *

Studio Focus: Conversations from the Classroom
ZOOM! ZOOM! ZOOM!

INT. CLASSROOM—DAY

MARGIE
My Fearful Child was concerned about doing my weekend intensive on Zoom. The night before, it was in full crazy mode. "How am I going to do this workshop on Zoom? I can't hug anyone. We can't be near one another. How can you be an actor and not physically connect? And how the hell am I going to guide them through an emotional trust exercise when I'm not by their side? Ugh!" Two people backed out. Everyone else wanted to as well, but we somehow convinced them to stay.

To my astonishment, it was one of the best weekends I have ever led! Each skeptical actor discovered the advantages of being on Zoom. There is an intense focus on the individual who is talking at any particular moment. We have an unobstructed view of all their thoughts and behavior. I calmed my Critical Parent and Fearful Child. My Adult declared, "Trust your ability and know they will learn enormously from you." My Nurturing Parent poured these words over me: "I am so proud of you for taking this on. I love you. You are amazing." And my Playful Child chimed in with, "Go, girlfriend! You love living in the unknown. Fuck it! *And forgive yourself for your doubt!*"

Lisa, what have you gone through this week while facing the challenges of the coronavirus?

LISA

In working on this slice this week, I did what you suggested. I took walks and continued to create. And then yesterday, I got into my Critical Parent who said: "You don't know what you are doing. You have to be off-book and know your lines. Have you done enough work on this?" Those voices were getting in my way, so I had to have a conversation with myself this morning about trusting my own sense of humanity. In doing so, I talked myself off the ledge.

MARGIE

It is so great that you went through that. It is going to happen in the real world. You are going to feel great. You can feel your Playful Child winning out, and then you can be hit with fear. But now, you can remind yourself that you have gone through this doubt before. It's good to fall down so you can find ways to lift yourself up that are healthier.

JEN

All these self-tape challenges are happening now because this coronavirus has closed the industry of auditioning. So, I had to write a monologue or a scene for a casting director, and my Critical Parent screamed at me: "You're not a good writer. They're not even going to watch it. It's a waste of your time." The Adult said: "You have no idea if that is true. Creating is the right thing to do, and you feel accomplished when you finish."

And I got out of it with my Playful Child saying: "Oh, my gosh, this is so much fun. Why don't you write some more?"

MARGIE

Good for you, Jen! Who else wants to share?

TAYLOR

I was having the same challenge that Jen was having. I saw all these monologue challenges, and I had never posted anything like that. I was hesitant about it, but after class last week, I was so inspired that I decided to take the risk. I did it spontaneously and felt playful, but when I went to post it, my Fearful Child freaked out. "Maybe it's not good enough to post. I think it's too boring. I'll just post it the next day." And the next day, my Fearful Child was still in control. It took me four days to post it. I had to activate my Nurturing Parent to say it was okay, and summon my Adult to find out why I was afraid to share it. I felt too vulnerable to put myself out there, but I said, "This is for you. Not for anyone else." I posted it and celebrated that I took that chance.

MARGIE

That's a victory for you! You know, Taylor, you have really improved in your five voices by taking action. You may have had the Critical Parent and Fearful Child telling you that you're not good enough, but your Playful Child won out. Bravo.

R.D.

I'm the opposite of Jen and Taylor. I never got there this week. I was excited about creating, and then life kicked in—dealing with my kids' online school, and then technical issues with our frickin' internet. My son is nine, and my daughter is twelve. I'm managing their schedules while my wife is working full-time at home. Pushing away my creativity, I stopped taking care of myself. "You don't have time to create. You have to take care of your kids. What are you thinking?" Then I would go back to my Nurturing Parent, who would say, "Enjoy yourself. You deserve time to be creative. It's what you love." But then I would argue with myself by saying, "You are a screwup! You can't handle it. You will be terrible in class!"

MARGIE

So, what is the main thing you have to do during this time?

R.D.

I have to push through it and say, *fuck it!*

MARGIE

Yes, that too. But it starts with a different F. Anyone know it? (Silence)
The other magic word is "forgiveness." This is a difficult time. You have to be a father. A husband. A creator. It's challenging. I suggest making your goals realistic. Maybe you won't be able to memorize the slice. Maybe you won't be able to spend as much time with this script as you would have wanted. And you know what, R.D.? That's okay.

SALLY

I cut all my hair off. My husband used to cut hair. So, I thought, "Yeah, I'm gonna do it. What do I need all this hair for? Go for it!" That was my Playful Child taking risks. But when it came time to do it, I was terrified.

MARGIE

So, you had to deal with the Fear and Critical Parent who is always commenting, "I have to look good. If I don't look good, I won't make it in this world. It's all about my appearance. No one will want to see me if I have short, ugly hair!" But you took the risk and removed all the hair that was, by the way, making it easier for you to hide your face. It was a really bold move, and I applaud you for taking that chance.

SALLY

Thanks. Last week, I did so much creation—went so far into that rabbit hole. This week was more, "You know what? You've got this. You don't have to push so hard. Just let go and trust that you own her." I realized it's my fucking class, my fucking hair. I am doing this for me. It's my opportunity. I did a meditation this morning where I lay on the floor, put my hand on my heart, and repeated, "I love you. I love you." I think about all my good qualities and give to myself what I give to other people.

MARGIE

Sally, that makes me want to cry. What a great example of using your Nurturing Parent by giving yourself the love you deserve. You recognized your own awesomeness. We all do.

EUGENIA

I did two stand-up shows on Zoom, and I was terrified. I felt so vulnerable, and not having an audience was really a challenge. But I jumped into the space in front of my camera, had a blast, and just really had to trust that it would work out.

MARGIE

The thing about trust is you trust yourself first, and then you can trust everything and everyone around you. So, Massi, how is our handsome Italian actor doing today?

MASSI

I have been doing really well. I have found that I am using my Adult more than ever. I have to set up structure for myself. I concentrate on my studies, work out, eat well, and go out every day and take a walk. I am not working, but it was an opportunity for me to study English and bring out both my Adult and Playful Child.

STARLA

I ride my bike every day. It keeps my head clear and allows me to have my own special time with me. My Nurturing Parent is present during that time. I worked on my lines and felt good, and now that I'm here, I am nervous and fearful.

MARGIE

I keep reminding all of you that nerves are part of human behavior. It's okay to be nervous. You all are human beings. You can acknowledge that it is okay to be nervous. If you drop your lines, you drop your lines. It's a moment of forgiveness.

BRYCE

This has not been a great week for me. I'm in a rut. Mental health—depression—it takes me three hours to get out of bed. But I tricked myself into moving forward. I told myself this class is what makes me feel alive.

MARGIE

Yes, it's really important that your Nurturing Parent guide you by saying: "My darling Bryce, it may be a bad day, but there is always tomorrow. Things will get better." By coming to class, you already have a win. You need to label the voices and say to the Fearful Child, "I am not leaving you alone. You are just a piece of me. I am not leaving you. I am going to take care of you this week." Vocalize it as if you are conversing with a dear friend.

Thanks, everyone. What I love about this class is your courage and extraordinary willingness to grow. You inspire me.

I've missed more than nine thousand shots in my career. I've lost almost three hundred games. Twenty-six times, I've been trusted to take the game-winning shot and missed. I've failed over and over and over again in my life. And that is why I succeed.

—Michael Jordan, former professional
basketball player and businessman

Christian Hicks's Story— Open to the Chaos

Last month, I worked on a movie in Atlanta. It was scheduled to shoot in twenty days. It got shot in ten. The coronavirus lockdown literally came to Los Angeles on the last day of shooting. Needless to say, it was disorganized, and people were complaining. Even actors were freaking out on set. I kept to my path and knew, no matter what, I only had one job, which was to keep creating and do the best I could while having fun in the process. All that other stuff and stress was "not my job."

For me, the whole Critical Parent thing has now come to a place of understanding, acceptance, and self-love. Would I want a friend or lover walking around with me all day making negative comments all the time, especially when I am doing the thing I love? No. No! I have broken up with that state of mind.

Last but not least, in all the above, I claim progress on letting go of perfection and remembering to laugh. Something I learned when I was sentenced to prison for eight years at age seventeen was that I have to make the best of what I have. Tough times teach trust. If I can continue to create now, there are all kinds of possibilities. I am open to all the chaos. It will pass. I will live each day with gratitude.

Everything you want is on the other side of fear.

—Jack Canfield, author and motivational speaker

Studio Focus: **Conversations from the Classroom**
TASTE OF NORMALCY

INT. CLASSROOM—DAY

MARGIE

Good morning, my wonderful Wednesday class. What were you aware of this past week regarding your five voices, and what actions did you take to be healthier?

NIKKO

I'm in a weird headset. I never procrastinate, and yet this week, I didn't want to do anything. My Critical Parent gets pissed at me and says, "You are bad." I'm not used to it. I meditate, and then two hours later, I'm back into that negative space. It's hard to find the balance.

MARGIE

It is a balance. The Critical Parent is going to return. It is inside you. You may quiet it for a while, but other times it will come out, and you have to be okay with it. Does that make sense?

a drive
Balance

MADALYN

My Fearful Child came out this week. "What if I never get to work again? What if I don't get to live a full life?" So, I have been journaling more. The second it happens, I sprint upstairs and jot it down. And if that isn't enough, I will lie in bed and do what you taught me—hug myself through my Nurturing Parent. Then I'll go hang out with my sister.

MARGIE

I love the way Maddie came up with so many solutions. That is a good use of your Adult. It really is shifting the lens from the out of control, Fearful or Critical voices. You have to take action.

ADAM

My Fearful Child is trying to memorize the monologue that the casting directors want us to do. And then I say, what is the point? I will memorize it and submit it like thousands of other actors are doing now, and then who is going to do what with it? Why work on that instead of doing something fun? So I bought some hot dogs, relish, and mustard, and fired up the grill like when I was a kid. I just gave myself a taste of normalcy. It was like crack! It felt so good! Treating myself in some way that is human is wonderful. I also watched Richard in *Clemency* and was so proud of him.

MARGIE

I love a taste of normalcy.

DOUG

I reviewed the notes from class. I find myself more self-observant now. I am aware of my procrastination, so I focus more. But I don't know what voice that is.

MARGIE

So, what ego state/voice would that be?

DOUG

Would that be my Adult?

MARGIE

Bingo! Yes, that would be your Adult that is giving you some answers to get better.

DOUG

I did some "adulting" today and some landscaping.

NERIDA

You are all speaking my language. I keep looking at my anxiety. I have a full-on schedule, because I needed order. I wanted to be productive every day, but now I have overdone it. I'm overwhelmed with all that I am doing. Writing my series, reading two plays, or planning when I do my exercise. The knot of anxiety is because I am not allowing myself to chill.

MARGIE

Your structure has been great. That is your Adult. What you need to give to yourself is more of your Playful Child. "I'm going to enjoy eating popcorn, watching a movie, and eating that chocolate bar that is sitting in the refrigerator with my name on it!" Breathing, meditating, and watching TV is helpful for me. It is looking at the balance.

FROM OVERWHELMED TO POWERFUL

It's easy to get overwhelmed by everything we feel we need to do or should do. When we say "should" to ourselves, we are letting the Critical Parent run the show.

It's important to remember that creativity is stymied by criticism.

The following exercise is something that can be done anywhere and only takes minutes, but it will change the track of your thinking from feeling overwhelmed to feeling personally powerful. Gratitude opens the mind to receive even more.

MARGISM: CONNECT TO THE FIVES

Without censoring your own thoughts, write down:
 Five things that you like about yourself.
 Five things that you did well today.
 Five things for which you are grateful.
 Gratitude is an action, so say "thank you" three times.

Pen work

Love yourself first and everything else falls
into line. You really have to love yourself
to get anything done in this world.

—Lucille Ball, comedian, actress, and producer

Studio Focus: Conversations from the Classroom
"PLEASE DON'T PUT ME IN ANGELA BASSETT'S LIGHT!"

INT. CLASSROOM–DAY

MARGIE
When do your Fearful Child and Critical Parent come out in acting, and what can you do to help lower those voices?

CHELSEA
I was on set. I felt very confident but missed the opportunity to be more playful with it. When I came home, I was so critical of myself, but then I turned it around by using my breath as a prescription. I inhaled and followed it up to the crown of my head, then exhaled and followed it down my spine.

[handwritten margin note: Breath exercise]

MARGIE
So, you used your Adult to help you with your Critical Parent by using a specific breath exercise. What other voice could you listen to?

CLASS IN UNISON
The Nurturing Parent!

MARGIE
When you are feeling horrible, talk kindly to yourself with a sweet, vulnerable tone versus the Adult's tone.

CHELSEA
At the first audition I booked after the master weekend, I noticed a huge difference after the intensive. I felt empowered and wasn't stressed in the waiting room. My "scene" was with the great Angela Bassett, and I think I'm ready, but then I see this powerful icon, and my Fearful Child and Critical Parent start yelling inside of me. "OMG, I'm not experienced enough, I'm going to fuck this up, I'm not ready to do these three complicated scenes." And to make it more terrifying, Angela says to the

director, "She is going to be in my light." And I'm thinking, "Please don't put me in her light." But then I let it go and felt pretty good about it. Of course, doubt crept in as I drove home, though, and questioned all the things I could have done better.

MARGIE

It is typical that whether it is an audition or an interview, we question whether we could have done better. It's the part of our brain that gets stuck in "I'm not enough." You have to shift the lens into looking at the pieces that you did well. "I am proud of what I did today," says the Nurturing Parent. The more you do that, the less you give power to the Critical Parent.

JOHNNO

When I go into an audition for an influential casting director, my Critical Parent is already there. "You have to do it right." But if I go into a free form show, I don't care, and my Playful Child is free. I need to let myself enjoy it and forget the business side of who I need to think I am talented.

MARGIE

We are controlled by the outcome. So, you are giving everyone the power but yourself. There is no fun, no joy. Change your perception to: "I don't care if it is a commercial, a short, or a movie, I am going to love it and let my Playful Child guide me." It is the journey, not the endgame. *It's the journey*   *Playful Child guide me*

BETSY

I was putting myself on tape. My Critical Parent started watching each take and criticizing it. I kept tweaking and tweaking and noticed that my freedom was gone. It was technically there, but the playfulness had disappeared. I really caught that after the fact.

MARGIE

Great that you caught it!

keep it I, not you . . .

DAKOTA

I would like to add something. Instead of saying, "This is hard," change it to, "It's an opportunity, it's exciting." Instead of walking into the room and saying, "Oh fuck," say "Fuck, yeah!" Find a positive alternative.

> *To love oneself is the beginning*
> *of a lifelong romance.*
>
> —Oscar Wilde, writer and gay provocateur

POWER CHALLENGE—PIECES OF YOURSELF

- Examine your Critical Parent. Write three different situations with people where that voice does not serve you.
- Most people think of the Critical Parent as strictly negative. Please write a time where it gave you some tough love that motivated you to go forward.
- Look at your Fearful Child. Describe three times when the Fearful Child has blocked your way to personal power and being the lead in your own life.
- The Fearful Child is often portrayed as a villain. But does the fearful child always have to be put in its place? When could you use your fear to fuel you?
- Describe the areas of your life that could use a good dose of the Nurturing Parent.
- When in your life has the Adult served you? Write three examples. Now write three examples of when it got in your way of being playful and creative.
- Enjoy writing down three different times where your Playful Child was loud and healthy.

6

Being Present

RACE AGAINST TIME

After five chapters, we arrive at where we are right now. Where are we? We are in the place where all the magic happens—the present moment.

When I was young, I never thought about being present. I simply was present. I didn't worry about the future, and I was too young to regret the past. I lived fully in the day I was in, absorbing everything. I was curious. I was available and open to discovery.

What does being available to discover allow us to do? It gives us an opportunity to stretch out each moment. If I rush my day, those seventeen waking hours shrink down to twelve.

HANGING WITH MARY

When I was twenty-two, I was singing in New York City, and as fate would have it, I met Mary Wilson from the Supremes. We started talking and instantly became friends. Two years later, Mary invited me to Las Vegas to celebrate the last show of Diana Ross & the Supremes. Of course, I went and had a blast.

Mary suggested that I move to Los Angeles and stay at her house with her. I took the risk, moving three thousand miles across the country, and thus began my adventure. Musicians like Dionne Warwick, the Temptations, the Four Tops, and even Michael Jackson stopped by her house, and we did something that is so foreign to me now—we would hang. Yes, we would hang out, lay by the pool, and just be. The minutes felt like hours, and the days felt like weeks. There was no race against time. Unless Mary was on tour, there was no need to get somewhere.

But that expansion of space ended when ambition became my focus. I became a mentor and then, some say, a legend in my profession. My life went from relaxed to fast forward. Often, I would catch up on calls while walking my dog and my neighbors would call out to me, "Get off the phone and just enjoy the walk!" I couldn't find the time to even do that.

When my mom was a hundred years old, she said to me, "How did I get to be this old?"

As any parent can tell you, and I found out when I adopted my son, it's a constant challenge to stay in the present. It doesn't seem to matter if our child is an infant, school age, or even an adult on his or her own. We worry about everything that could happen as well as every disaster we could fantasize about. Being present is elusive. I think I've got it, and it slips out of my hands.

The second I think I'm being present, I'm already dwelling on the past or racing into the future. If I take a few breaths, feel the sun on my face, listen to the birds sing, smell the crisp autumn air, I feel grounded. This is the true answer to happiness and something I am forever refining. It's a work in progress, but so worth it.

Yesterday's the past, tomorrow is the future, but today is a gift. That's why it's called the present.

—Bill Keane, cartoonist, *The Family Circle*

LAGUNA WELLNESS RETREAT

I was suffering from fibromyalgia, which induces insomnia. I was advised to spend a week at a wellness retreat in Laguna. My willingness to take risks once again served me, but the exerience was not without its challenges. Seconds after arriving, I was outfitted with a CamelBak bag and heavy hiking boots. I was handed two poles (I thought I was going skiing!). It turns out a hike had been planned. At that moment, I realized I had bitten off more than I could chew. I was tempted to jump into my car and return to my safe, familiar home, but the adventurous part of me won out and I joined the young athletic group. Three hours later, after an exhausting hike, we ended up at the summit of a mountain. It felt like we were touching puffs of white magic moving freely through the sky. My exhaustion dissipated as I took a deep breath and beheld the picturesque countryside. All the stress in my body melted away; all the brain chatter vanished. For the first time, I understood the meaning of being present.

My favorite lunch at this retreat was a crisp, homemade Caesar salad. I never thought the smaller portions would be enough, and yes, I did want to lick the plate, but my taste buds had never experienced the joy of savoring each morsel. I spent most of the retreat in silence, reading, meditating, and just being. When I returned from this mindful week, I understood inner peace, loving myself, and staying in the moment. Whenever I feel overwhelmed, I remember those times of being present in Laguna.

MICROWAVE WORLD

How many times in my life have I given thanks to the microwave? Life just seems to be easier when you have shortcuts. We want things done quickly, and we don't have the patience to wait.

My grandmother made the best apple pie. As a child, I would go with her to a small market where the fruit was fresh and ripe. We would walk down the aisles, getting the ingredients to make the thin

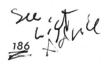
crust. We would sing songs while waiting patiently to pay. We would walk home, throwing beautifully autumn-colored leaves in her worn canvas bag to decorate the table. I was too young to cut the apples, but she let me use the rolling pin to smooth out her homemade crust. It felt like our time together would last forever. It's those memories of living in the moment with her that keep her alive in my heart. So, maybe the microwave doesn't help us as much as we think.

MARGISM

Be intimate with this moment, knowing it will never happen again.

* Bad Habits Are Hard to Break *

We all have bad habits that are difficult to break. Some habits are inconsequential. They might be annoyances, like not closing the cupboard doors, piling your clothes in a corner, or even staying up late to write a book. You can't break all your bad habits. But you can tackle ones that diminish your quality of life and prevent you from being present. When the bad habit feels like wearing a heavy coat on a summer day, it can be a burden. Take action to change them. I listed my bad habits and the actions I apply to change them.

High expectations	Be realistic
Rescuing	Stay in my own lane
Complaining/protesting	Zip it
Explaining	Less is more
Grabbing	Breathe
Speeding up	Slow down
Criticizing/judging	Kindness
Fearing/worrying	Let it go

Dr. Barbara Satinover's Story— The Burnt Toast Theory

My forty-seven-year-old daughter complains, "You know, Mom, from my childhood. . . ."

I interrupted her. "Enough with the childhood. It was decades ago. You have been holding on to this myth of who you are, and you need to learn how to do it differently. It's reached its expiration date."

Family

Most of us tend to live in the past. The truth is we have an automatic response to things from our childhood.

I made up this analogy—The Burnt Toast Theory.

If you grow up eating burnt toast, it is so familiar to you that if you are walking down the street and you smell burnt toast coming from someone else's home, you will go to their door. Even though it doesn't smell or taste good, you automatically go there without hesitation. You have to unlearn that impulse and say, "I am drawn to that smell, but it's not good for me." Instead, let me be here, in this present moment, smelling these beautiful flowers in my garden." That's the healthy place to be.

This thing you are worried about, the thing you are afraid of, it's not happening right now, at this very moment, is it? Then what are you worried about?

Worrying

—Dr. Barbara Satinover, marriage and family therapist

Studio Focus: **Conversations from the Classroom**
THE CURSE OF A CHAOTIC MIND

INT. CLASSROOM—DAY

KANDISS

With some people, I feel less than. I don't know why, but when I was younger, I would date guys who were either famous or rich, and I was never myself. After the date, I would ask myself, "Who am I?" I wouldn't talk. I was swallowed up. Not present.

With other people, I feel that I am my powerful self. I don't know how to bring that part of me around those who intimidate me.

MARGIE

When we give power to another person, we become powerless. When I think this person is better than me, I feel smaller. But through empathy and curiosity for others whom I might find difficult, I am able to be kinder and more present.

BRYCE

I realize I spend 98 percent of my time worrying about the future or harping about the past. I forget that there is a now and feel so sad that another day of my life has gone by, and I hadn't lived in it. I missed the sunset. Didn't look at the flowers. Didn't take this moment in.

MARGIE

I can see all of you in this Zoom class shaking your heads. Where did it go? I go to sleep, and I think another day has gone by. I feel like a day is a blink of an eye.

JAMES

I am struggling every day. The only thing that helps me is to drink. I am too afraid to stay present.

MARGIE

Yes, drinking is a way to stuff your feelings in so you don't have to feel them. But it is a temporary fix. Every time you stuff your fear inside of you, it will eventually come out in ways that are unhealthy. We have been taught that if we don't look at it, it will go away. Being present lets you feel those feelings without attaching an outcome. To be present, you have to be brave enough to sit in those difficult feelings. Then you can forgive yourself, go have one drink or an ice cream sundae.

SALLY

I've suffered from depression and anxiety my whole life. I'm realizing that they're learned behaviors from the past. It's a habit. I am used to feeling a certain way. So, when I wake up in the morning, I ask immediately, "Where is my anxiety? Oh, there it is." When you look for it, you find it. So, this week, I caught myself going back to that habit. And I said, "Hold on a minute. That is from the past, and the past ain't good for me no more!"

MARGIE

Well said, Sally! The past, at times, is a horror flick that we watch over and over again. You can't become the lead in your own life if you are living in your past.

> *The past has no power*
> *over the present moment.*

—Eckhart Tolle, spiritual teacher and self-help author

Therapy Session—Catch the Impulse

MARGIE

Two nights ago, I had a dream that I had lung cancer. I struggle with staying present when it comes to my fear of dying and my health.

THERAPIST

That's more of a nightmare.

MARGIE

That was a nightmare. Susan reminded me, "Remember, you have fibromyalgia, and it transfers into different parts of your body." I have unusual symptoms that aren't necessarily connected to a disease but are connected to symptoms of fibromyalgia. So, I want to work on that. I want to talk about that.

THERAPIST

And what do you want from working on it and talking about it?

MARGIE

I want to put those thoughts in a small box, not into a place of catastrophic behavior.

THERAPIST

Well, apparently, you have in the past, but we're challenging that bad habit in the future.

MARGIE

When I'm walking down the street, and I start to feel like I can't breathe, at that moment, I have to shift from my habit of being catastrophic—I can't breathe, so I must have lung cancer.

THERAPIST

So, mindfulness training is your supporter here. One Buddhist habit is to name the pattern of the mind. And you do it by naming it three times, and if you can do it in a singsong manner, it's better. So, "Meaning, meaning, meaning."

MARGIE

Oh, so it helps to name the pattern of my mind, "Fearing, fearing, fearing."

THERAPIST

So, let's walk down the street, and all of a sudden, your lungs aren't working optimally.

MARGIE

I'm walking down the street, and I'm noticing my body, my lungs.

THERAPIST

One thing to know about lungs, though, is they're connected to the emotion of fear because it's your survival instinct. If your elbow hurts, you're not going to have elbow cancer. Right?

MARGIE

Right.

THERAPIST

I want you to catch the impulse. Now, we're going to capitalize on observing and noticing, please.

MARGIE

So, I'm walking down the street. I'm noticing my body, and in my body are my lungs. And in my lungs, I noticed that my breath is shorter.

THERAPIST

Yeah. And let your eyes look around. Your eyes are a neurological resource. The eyes are determining whether someone has a gun at your head, a knife at your throat, or if a saber-toothed tiger is coming to eat you.

MARGIE

Or it's beautiful out, and the sun is shining. And the leaves are moving, and there's color.

THERAPIST

Then what do you think I'm going to want you to notice?

MARGIE

My breathing.

THERAPIST

Yes.

MARGIE

My body is still constricted. My lungs feel constricted.

THERAPIST

Let's go after that old bad habit for you to observe and notice it. "Oh my God, I must have lung cancer."

MARGIE

Okay.

THERAPIST

And then let me hear you observe.

MARGIE

I'm observing what the mind did. The mind went into a catastrophic place.

THERAPIST

Now, make a drama out of it. Aren't you in the Hollywood industry?

MARGIE

I decided to write my own movie about death when I took a holiday.

THERAPIST

No. You wrote a movie where you starred in an Oscar-winning performance. You're going to need a subchapter on becoming the lead in a horror movie or a suspense sci-fi drama.

MARGIE

So true.

THERAPIST

With a Shakespearian tragic ending.

MARGIE

Fabulous.

THERAPIST

Okay. So, now let me hear you practice naming that feeling three times: name, name, name.

MARGIE

Okay. "Drama, drama, drama."

THERAPIST

Look what your eyes did.

MARGIE

Opened up.

THERAPIST

And you looked around.

MARGIE

Which helps keep me from getting stuck in myself.

THERAPIST

Yes. You've compared your internal Hollywood movie, scriptwriting drama with the drama of the beautiful trees, the light, the flowers, or the day. There was a comparison your brain did, but it breaks the habit.

MARGIE

It's looking at each piece of the puzzle in an objective way so I can change the bad habit of being reactive. Being the Adult allows me to have a cognitive process. Therefore, I can stay present. And remain sane!

> We're so busy watching out for
> what's just ahead of us that we don't
> take time to enjoy where we are.
>
> —Bill Watterson, cartoonist and author of
> the comic strip *Calvin and Hobbes*

* What's Your Relationship with Relationships? *

THE PITCH

A real estate company hired me to help their agents with listing presentations. Ten agents, both experts and rookies, attended this one-day workshop. I had asked them to prepare their presentation before the meeting.

I set up an exercise: The scenario was for two people, an agent and a homeowner, to act out a pitch. Armed with her presentation, the first agent entered the imaginary home and spouted off her experience, launching into her marketing plan for the home with an overabundance of statistics. Lost in her own thoughts, she barely engaged with the person playing the owner. She wasn't available to pick up any cues from the seller, because she wasn't at all present. We could all feel her desperation, stuck in her leather-bound presentation, which came from being in a sales drought. She wasn't at all curious about the homeowner. Curiosity allows us to be open to a conversation. It allows us to be present with our listener.

The next agent who participated in this improvisation was new to the game. Her fear was apparent. I don't think she took even one breath during her entire pitch.

"Hi. I'm Marlene. Oh my god, I love this house! I love this area. I have always wanted to live here. Of course, I couldn't afford this place. Most people can't. The schools alone cost a fortune. My child was on the tennis team, which used to play against Brentwood. What a fabulous school that is! Jesse goes to a public school. Not that it is a bad school. It just doesn't give you the same education and opportunities." And on. And on. And on.

Marlene was like a deer in the headlights. She couldn't see anything in front of her.

I had her start all over again, but this time taking a big breath before entering the house. I had her use her imagination as if she were truly in this house, so she could experience it and share with the class as many details as she could, starting with the seller.

"I'm taking a breath. I am entering his living room, and the seller is in front of me. He has thick dark hair with gray strands by his temples, eyes as blue as the ocean, and a welcoming smile with extraordinary white teeth."

"Slow down," I tell her. "Don't tell the story. Experience what you see. Being present requires you to breathe and pause, allowing time for the other person to share."

She continues, "I notice a woven basket, a wooden lamp, and a large abstract painting with pastel colors. I take another breath and feel my feet on the floor and the cool air in the house."

"That's a great way of centering yourself, Marlene," I praised. *Grounding exercise* "Now you are ready to begin, because you have taken the attention off of you. The most important part of being present is being silent. Listen. Observe. You don't have to speak all the time."

At the end of the class, they left with the keys to being in the present. Each of these following seven steps can become a small victory to becoming the lead in your own life, no matter what life path you walk. *Centering exercise* *Being Present*

1. Start with a breath.
2. Check out the likable details of the other person.
3. Take time to observe the surroundings.
4. Listen and take cues from the other person.
5. Ask open-ended questions, allowing him to reveal his concerns.
6. Don't be afraid of silence.
7. Enjoy the conversation. It's the relationship that keeps us present.

Studio Focus: **Conversations from the Classroom**
MY DOG IS A GAME-CHANGER FOR MY LIFE

INT. CLASSROOM—DAY

IZZY

My dog is a game-changer for my daily life. I could be crying, and she would start growling at me. I would say, "Wow, what was that behavior?" and when my mom saw her doing that, she told me my dog was trying to get me out of that Victim mindset. My dog senses it. She just knows. There is this beautiful being right in front of me, and I have to step out of that negative space and be with her.

MARGIE

That's beautiful. The relationship with your dog keeps you present. Dogs are great listeners. Listening is a true art.

BROOKE

I find the present elusive. I would like to find a way to be present, even if I don't trust the person in front of me.

MARGIE

I understand. It is so much easier to be present if you trust the other person. The way to be present, even if you don't trust the other person, is to trust yourself. The answer to being present is to not run away from those feelings you have—fear, sadness and pain. Sit with them. When you meditate and go deeper into those feelings, you can find your inner strength and peace.

JP

Being present is all about listening and focusing. In a scene, if I look at the room and touch a chair, it grounds me, and I don't think about my lines.

MARGIE

Yes, by touching your skin, feeling your feet on the floor, or touching the objects near you, it will ground you. But when you are with another person, the best thing is to focus on the parts of that person in front of you—their eyes, skin, hair, smile—all of that will keep you in the moment.

MELANIE

My phone controls me. The need to stay in touch with everyone is perpetually jerking me out of the present moment. It's a fucking nightmare.

MARGIE

OMG. I am obsessed with my phone. I don't think I can go more than a half-hour without checking my emails, texts, and voicemail. It is the most distracting object in my life. My son recently said not to call him for two days as he was unplugging. I was quite impressed.

FEAR IS YOUR ALLY

How can you be present when you live in uncertainty? It stops us from moving forward. We default back to what makes us feel safe and lose the desire to explore the unknown.

Fear can become the focus of your life, especially if you've been in unstable situations while growing up or even as an adult. We may think that earning more money, getting the gig, moving to a gated community, checking our health every day, and staying in our self-made cocoon of protection will make our fears subside. Not true. One fear is exchanged for a different fear. People who make a lot of money become terrified of losing it. You get the acting gig and become terrified of failing. Your fear affects your health by giving you anxiety. When fear rules your life, the decisions you make become burdens or regrets.

The key is to use your fear as an ally. Let it challenge you to move forward in your life. It can motivate you to take risks. In my life, when I break down that wall of fear, I find that it helps me with the next moment. It instills the courage to embrace new challenges and revel in the joy of being present.

We can easily manage if we will only take,

each day, the burden appointed to it.

But the load will be too heavy for us if we

carry yesterday's burden over again today,

and then add the burden of the morrow

before we are required to bear it.

—John Newton, cleric and a captain of
slave ships before becoming an abolitionist

* Come to Your Senses! *

THE BODY KEEPS US PRESENT

It is hard to stay present when fear snowballs through the body. Recognize what is happening by tracking what is going on in the body—gut, chest, breath, anywhere you feel sensations of fear. It keeps me in the present.

When I have a thought that takes me away from this moment, whether it is regret of the past or fear of the future, I put my attention on how my body is reacting. I acknowledge that my shoulders are lifted, my chest is tight, my teeth are clenched, and my breath is short. By naming exactly what is going on in my body, I can stay in the observation state. Once I have observed it, then I let my body fix it. My body is smart. I don't have to intervene and tell it to take a breath. I accept that the breath is simultaneously voluntary and involuntary. That is how I stay in the present, by letting my body do the work. When I tell my body to breathe, I am intervening, but if I stay present, then it will go away on its own. It slows everything down. The fear and anxiety may be there, but I get to sort it out cause I am not trying to fix it. It is in my best interest to accept the fear, be at peace with it.

Studio Focus: **Conversations from the Classroom**
AN AVOCADO CAN BE A WHOLE WORLD

INT. CLASSROOM–DAY

MARGIE
How do you help yourself to be present?

KELLY
I come back to my body by being physical. I stretch, touch my skin, feel the air on my skin, and see what is in the room.

KEELIA
I run on rocks, which may sound painful, but it makes me present because, if I'm not in the moment, I could really hurt myself. I'm breathing a lot, and I'm saying don't die!

MARGIE
So, it is about experiencing all of your senses. What is most challenging for you to not be in the present?

KELLY
I think, when I am working from home and juggling with my personal life, I get overwhelmed. I'm not going anywhere because they are all happening at the same time.

MADALYN
I find it hard to stay present when I get overwhelmed. I have known you for a long time, and you have always talked about breath, which has stuck with me. If I give myself permission to center myself through breath, I can get back to being present.

MARGIE
Breathing happens without us paying any attention to it. When we call attention to it, watch it, and experience it fully, we stay present. Taking a deep breath centers us.

KIMBERLEY

When I think about being present, I think about being an observer and not letting my ego get in the way. It's about being truly open and being in the middle of the light and the dark, the yin and the yang.

MARGIE

I was so stressed out after doing eight hours of Zooming that I went outside and really looked at a tree that has been in my backyard for twenty-three years. I felt like I was looking at it for the first time. I always knew the tree was there but never saw the different colors of the leaves, the thickness of the trunk, and the beauty as it swayed in the wind. It's just slowing down by using all of our senses—the sights, sounds, touch, taste, and smells—all of them will extend our moments of pleasure.

ADAM

I found one of my favorite paintings and sent it to one of those paint-by-numbers companies. It's gratifying to paint one of your favorite pictures, even if you're not a great artist.

NIKKO

I use my imagination, with my senses, to visualize what my future is like. I don't think about it. I find that it doesn't make me panic. Then, I open my eyes and use all my senses to be here in the moment.

RUSHI

I meditate in the morning. I put a timer on for fifteen minutes, and it makes me happy and stills my mind.

RICHARD

What helps me is to boil fresh ginger, which in itself helps a lot, and drink it as a tea. It's soothing to the nervous system.

MARGIE

If you struggle being present, try this: Find something you love to eat—see it, touch it, smell it, taste it, and listen to the sounds of eating it. Enjoy it. A slice of avocado can be a whole world. You will find that you have taken the first step to be in the present.

> *We make mistakes; we cannot turn*
> *the clock back and try again.*
> *All we can do is use the present well.*
>
> —The Dalai Lama

Irina Kompa's Story—
Lift Up My Head and Look at the Sky

What takes me away from being present is remembering all the things I have to do. Why am I rushing through life? I decided to take this time and enjoy working on an English accent instead of worrying about my Russian one. I am doing this for myself.

When I get preoccupied with thoughts of what is next, I step outside, lift my head, and look at the sky. I take a moment to really see the sky, the color of it. Then the smell of a fresh breeze hits my senses, and I just breathe it in. I stop and look around, not just look at flowers, people, trees, but also really see them, their colors, and their beauty. Then all my body fills up with an amazing sense of freedom, happiness in this particular moment—that's for me. When I am able to hear the sound of birds, I am in the present. Later, I pick up a pen and paper and write without thinking, just three pages, whatever pops into my mind. I put it away without reading it. Then I breathe, and I have released my anxiety.

Ha! Ha!.

For fast-acting relief, try slowing down.

—Lily Tomlin, actress, comedian, singer, and producer

* Acceptance—
The Sister of Being Present *

Sandy Gomper's Story—
A Unique Woman with a Unique Perspective

MARGIE

I have known you since I was a kid. You were friends with my sister, Lois. I can remember at Camp Kear Sarge, when you were walking back from dinner, all dressed up, and decided to jump off the dock in the lake. All the girls in our bunk, including my sister, watched in awe and asked, "What the hell were you doing?"

And you replied: "Why not? It's not a big deal."

I have admired you so much for your willingness to let go and live in the present. I know you had your own demons to overcome. Tell me about who you used to be and how you tackle life now.

SANDY

My struggle with anger started when I was very young. My childhood was lonely. My parents did not know how to bring up a kid. And years ago, when I was married, I was constantly filled with anger. I lived with a man who kept a secret about his childhood. He was a Holocaust victim who never shared the experience of surviving the war and never shared that he was adopted till much later in our marriage, which made him live in deep depression. So, the combination of a depressed human and an angry one was not a good combo.

MARGIE

So, how did you survive?

SANDY

I became independent and wasn't afraid of moving forward. I realized I was the only one who could help myself, and I started to see life as beautiful. Fear doesn't control me.

MARGIE

Most people have a fear of relationships, fear of illness, fear of death, and so on. What do you do with your fear?

SANDY

I don't think of any of it. I accept what is. I have gone through many years without a relationship. Do I wish I had one? Absolutely. Having a partner is fabulous. But I don't. So, it's acceptance. I have to accept myself first. And accept what life puts down for you and try to navigate what's there.

MARGIE

When we go to sleep at night, most of us are kept awake by fears that pop into our brains. What about you?

SANDY

When I go to sleep, I think of all the people I love, and the joys of all the places I have visited.

MARGIE

You stay positive and present.

SANDY

I don't have fear. Have I experienced things that were bad? Absolutely. But I have gotten through it. I feel blessed.

MARGIE
So, you feel grateful?

SANDY
I am grateful for everything. Grateful for my friends.
Grateful for my children. I am not handicapped by illness. I
can get up every day and move forward. Grateful for the
beauty of my life.

MARGIE
I am curious about our recent discussion on how you don't
need anyone else to make you happy. How does that work?

SANDY
I am happy within myself.

MARGIE
I'm also fascinated by your lack of stress. I don't understand
that. I have so much stress.

SANDY
When I let go, I find peace within myself. I feel blessed, so I
don't go down that road. I travel down the road of purpose
for myself. Last week, I found purpose in making a great
soup. I brought it to my kids. It made me feel good. It made
them feel good.

MARGIE
So, it's the little things.

SANDY
It's the little things. You have to nourish yourself, and then
you can give it back.

MARGIE
It seems to me it's all about seeing the butterflies and being
present.

SANDY

I am a realistic person as well. If I find something I don't like, I ask myself, how do I get through this? You have to be present. Worry is about tomorrow. I'm not in tomorrow. I might not even be here tomorrow. The past is gone.

MARGIE

Let go and stay present.

MICHAEL JORDAN—MICRO-FOCUSED

Most people spend years trying to be present. They do yoga. Retreats. Meditation. Not Michael Jordan. He seemed to always be present, never anywhere else. His gift was being completely present, and that separated him from any other player. If other players were thinking about failure, he was not. Michael didn't let that get in his head.

"Why would I think about missing a shot I didn't take yet?" Jordan said during a press interview.

Michael Jordan was an ambassador for the United States. He changed the culture of sports. If you were lucky enough to see him play, you witnessed a man who knows how to stay in the moment, even to the last minute of his final game.

Jordan didn't seem stressed out that Scottie Pippen was injured. He had already missed twenty shots, but he just focused on each moment, one after another. At the end of his fourteen-year journey as a Chicago Bull, he remained completely present.

When the Bulls ended their season in 1998, the team put all their emotions onto pieces of paper, and without reading them, they burned all of them in a flaming trash can. There were no regrets. It ended with the incredible connection that only a six-time NBA championship could have. Without his complete commitment to being in the moment, Michael Jordan would not have been the best of the best.

(*Only put off until tomorrow what you
are willing to die having left undone.*

—Pablo Picasso, artist

Studio Focus: **Conversations from the Classroom**
MEDITATION

INT. CLASSROOM—DAY

MARGIE
It's up to us to be happy, to feel better. Meditation, once
you find the right form for yourself, can help you be present.
So, can you describe to me a meditation style that works
for you?

LISA
I think I have attention deficit disorder, so being present is
challenging. I discovered meditation. Even before the audition,
I will breathe and get in my body.

NIKKO
I use this app called *Balance*. It has a plan that is all about love
and kindness toward a challenging person that you love. And,
finally, toward yourself. I just finished one this morning, and I
gave myself some love.

RICHARD
There's the theory that there are multiple universes
(multiverses) and that this is not the only one. And there are
infinite versions of you. So, anything that you can imagine is
real in another parallel universe. When I meditate, I float there
and connect to anyone and everyone to receive guidance if I
need it. I find it helpful and centering.

TYLER

I use the app *Headspace,* and it dives into mindfulness. When I realize I am not connecting to my breath, I forgive myself and go back to meditation. And I saw this video that talks about expanding mindfulness to everything you do—mindful when washing dishes, arguing with your spouse, or as many things that I can throughout the day.

LINC

My wife has taught me to practice gratitude. If I focus on all that I am thankful for—a great day with my wife or a moment with my dog—then the rest of the day is joyful, but if I let myself spiral into fear of the unknown, then the rest of the day is shitty. I stop myself and say, "Hey, you have a roof over your head and a wonderful wife." That helps propel me forward.

MARGIE

The key for me is forgiveness. Forgiving when I am not present. I have the best life because I get to teach all of you, but the next day, I will forget that, and I want to kick myself for being unappreciative. Then I realize it is human, and I accept my imperfections.

KIMBERLEY

I'm a big meditation nerd. I'm far down the rabbit hole of yoga. To me, it's about appreciating daily life, learning how to actually enjoy waiting for the bus. It's all so simple. It's not like doing psychedelics.

MARGIE

You are absolutely right. It's all so simple. Here's a thought for the whole class: What if we all let in 1 percent more love and happiness every day?

When I'm in a situation and can't step away to meditate or ground myself, this exercise has become my favorite method to get back to the present. Smoking an imaginary cigarette allows me to shift my attention so that I don't come from a reactive place. Instead, it brings me into a space of calm.

It's important to follow the instructions below to get the greatest benefit out of this exercise.

MARGISM:
SMOKE YOUR IMAGINARY CIGARETTE

1. With your eyes closed, begin with two fingers on your right or left hand and gently touch your lips as you take in a slow, deep inhale while moving your imaginary cigarette from your lips elegantly.
2. Open your eyes as you slowly exhale. Watch the imaginary smoke as it moves from the right side all the way to the left side of your space until all the "smoke" is out of your lungs.
3. Stay, pause, in that quiet moment, in the present, enjoying the peace it brings to you.
4. Smile for yourself.

Eugenia Kuzmina's Story— From Russia, with Love

Being vulnerable and being present are both a necessity. My personal experience with these two qualities is a journey. In post-Soviet Russia, we were taught in school to follow strict rules and color inside the lines or we would be punished and even beaten with rulers. I learned to hide my sensitivity and never express any feelings. Losing my dad at fifteen, I suddenly became the breadwinner for the family and turned into an overachiever. I was always on the go, accomplishing one job after another. In the modeling business, I learned to become a pleaser, just an object on which brands projected different messages. But my heart yearned to find my voice. Only after having kids did I learn that life is a miracle. My husband and I went to a silent retreat, and I fell in love with meditation and stillness. I took an improvisation class and learned the beauty of saying "yes" to the moment. In Margie's class, I learned, paradoxically, that having structure gives me the freedom to be messy. Now I'm messy. My kids are messy. We're all messy, present, and happy!

Studio Focus: Conversations from the Classroom
I WAS HAVING A MARGARITA ON MY BALCONY

INT. CLASSROOM—DAY

AMY
I was having a margarita on my balcony, and I put on some music from my home country, New Zealand. Then I Zoomed my family and brought on more family members until we had thirty of my cousins, aunts, and uncles join us. And it was fun and soothing. I felt like I freed my Playful Child, and I was able to stay present with all of them.

R.D.
I'm inherently shy. I have a hard time being seen, but I didn't when I was a kid until certain incidents occurred that changed me. I have issues with feeling good enough, smart, talented, or valued enough. I had a big call yesterday. When I was a kid, I was in the original cast of *Les Misérables*. And I hadn't connected with most of them for thirty years. It was on Zoom, and I was so intimidated that I barely spoke but then I

remembered what Margie taught me. I raised my Nurturing Voice and said, "That's okay. Everyone here probably feels the same way. They love you. You were a part of this family. They want to hear from you." It really helped. Suddenly, I dropped into the moment.

MARGIE

You know, R.D., I loved seeing you put your hand on your chest and physicalize the Nurturing Parent. Being present requires that voice. When you allow yourself to listen to the other person, you can't worry about yourself, and your fear subsides to let you live in the now. Listening is a powerful tool.

JACK

When I am writing music, I have to be listening to what I am writing; otherwise, I force the outcome, and the quality suffers.

MARGIE

You need to be in the now to grab that piece of creativity. We all know that when we are in fear, we spiral out. What helps you?

JACK

I breathe. I don't beat myself up. I say, "This too will pass." Then I sit back down and compose my music.

JEN

I love to do pottery. It isn't easy. If I am not present, I will fuck up the pot. A fucked-up pot is not a pretty sight!

GRABBING THAT BRASS RING—
IS IT WORTH IT?

The following slice of life is one I use in my acting classes. The character is giving advice to her friend, who is never happy in the moment.

"The future is overrated. I think a lot of people, including myself, make the mistake of expecting too much from life, that something ahead will make us feel complete."

"But you've got to have goals and dreams, right?"

"Of course, but what about making yourself happy in the present day-to-day? How often do you find yourself thinking that as soon as I have this job, or more money, or this car, or this person, then I'll be happy. There is something inherently wrong with that way of thinking. I think we set ourselves up for constant dissatisfaction."

When we worry about the future we cannot truly enjoy the present. What a powerful realization.

Therapy Session—"It's Just the Way I Like to Live"

THERAPIST

You're happy, right?

MARGIE

Yes, because I got good blood test results, which made me happy.

THERAPIST

"Because" answers fall into a trap. "Because I got laid, because I got a job, because I won the lottery, because I needed a new car, because I got a good report from the doctor."

MARGIE

So, "because" is from the outside, not from the inside?

THERAPIST

I'll be happy when I get a new car, when I get a clean health report from the doctor, when I get laid, when Friday at six o'clock comes. That's the future. So, what are you going to have until then? Misery.

MARGIE

So, even though I'm happy in the present, it's actually not living in the present, 'cause I say, "because" and "when."

THERAPIST

I'd like to upgrade it, and I'd like you to hear different answers.

MARGIE
Okay.

THERAPIST
I'm happy for no good reason. What are the conditions that
make you happy? No conditions. All right, another one. "Oh, it's
just a way to live."

MARGIE
Wow.

THERAPIST
Do you see, I'm not buying into the cause of what happened?

MARGIE
Happy is being. Being cheerful is your nature. That means 24/7
cheerfulness. I accept the challenge, but I am not quite there
yet. It's similar to what we talk about. I do not have a choice. I
am a loving, kind, warm person.

THERAPIST
Happy goes with it. Cheerful goes with it.

MARGIE
It's just the way I like to live.

THERAPIST
Yes. So, I was at Vons, and there were the cashier and
the bag boy, and I was in this mode. And I said, "I'm really
happy." And I could barely believe they were holding on to me
energetically; they liked it so much. They were like, "Oh, what
happened?" It's a setup. And I said, "Oh, no good reason. It's
just the way to live." And they burst, both of them just
exploded.

MARGIE
What a giving thing to do at this time of our lives.

THERAPIST

Suffering is the fruit of selfishness or a contracted ego. Joy awakens in the heart.

MARGIE

Wow.

THERAPIST

Margie? Why are you so happy? Look away, please. Don't look at me for a reaction.

MARGIE

It's just the way to live.

THERAPIST

Now that shrug was hugging yourself in it, so you're savoring it, but don't look back for feedback. I am asking you to live moment by moment in your life, Margie. And you have been way too enmeshed in others, and I'm trying to pull you out of that.

See, it's like when you smoke that imaginary cigarette, I've just got to watch how unbelievably phenomenal it is. And the joy I feel because you are absorbed in your experience. It's not selfish or self-centered or anything like that, nothing negative.

MARGIE

What happens to me when I smoke my imaginary cigarette is I believe, at that moment, that I have all the time to live that experience.

THERAPIST

Your whole life. And that's why that imaginary cigarette smoke is so captivating.

MARGIE

I don't care about your reactions or if you like me or not. I do this completely for myself. It's a simple movement of a serene, slow joy of being present. People are drawn to that.

THERAPIST

I am so captivated because I need it for myself. But the fingers and hands tell you another story. They're relaxed. The serene person isn't grabbing.

MARGIE

Don't grab it.

THERAPIST

When you move with femininity and presence, there's no grab.

MARGIE

It's all fluid.

THERAPIST

And it makes me relax because of it. And it's not that you're doing it to me. I'm relaxing because you are not grabbing. And that's why there are metaphors like the hungry lion at the African water hole. What do the animals do? Flee. But if the lion comes completely full, then animals won't necessarily run right away.

MARGIE

It's only the hungry lion that they are afraid of. Now I can add the response, "It's just the way I like to live," to my repertoire of ways to be happy and present. Thank you.

* Little Victories *

Studio Focus: Conversations from the Classroom
HOPE SETS US FREE

INT. CLASSROOM—DAY

MARGIE

We spend a lot of time thinking about all the difficulties going on in our lives, and we don't spend enough time celebrating the victories, the little victories. We need to slow down our process and enjoy those moments of triumph. We are so driven to achieve our goals with complete perfection and grab that brass ring that it's hard for us to appreciate the little things that need to be acknowledged. It doesn't have to be brass.

So, I want to open it up to a discussion of how you can look at your life right now through the lens of the six victories: taking risks to be seen, letting go of control, getting out of your comfort zone, removing your armor, getting out of the drama queen triangle, using our five ego states effectively, and being in the present.

Sometimes, if it's not a big victory, we don't even acknowledge it. It's the little victories that keep us healthy and make us feel better about ourselves. And in this class, one of the most important victories is finding our personal power. This has never been a typical acting class. It's a class of creating.

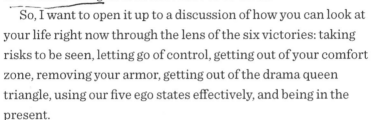

ADAM

I woke up a few times last night, afraid I was going to be late to class, and I still showed up on time.

MARGIE

Being on time is a victory for you!

ADAM

Yeah.

MARGIE

Does that feel good?

ADAM

Oh, yeah. I wanted to find a teacher who paid attention to me. And I didn't mean that they had a razor-sharp sense of when I was on time or not, but that they cared about me and we had a relationship. I have that with you through our conversations. It's a big win in the little victory category to have someone who knows a lot of my little personal tics and stuff and really pays attention, and that helps me look at myself kindly to make those changes.

MARGIE

When I look around this Zoom room, there's not one person I don't adore. And I think that's what makes it so beautiful. What other victories can we come up with that you can share with us? Rushi?

RUSHI

So, I have had a tumultuous relationship with my mother, and over the years, it has gotten worse. It was just so challenging, and it got to the point where it's the main reason I didn't come home. When I got married, however, we ended up staying with my mom. Over the span of time that I've been here, I've helped her with her home projects, and it feels like a small victory in our relationship.

MARGIE

You know, Rushi, relationships with families are always filled with struggles. I continue to learn the importance of constantly lowering my expectations toward people I love. They are complicated relationships. It's been like that the whole time. Unrealistic expectations make me unhappy. Forgiveness, acceptance, and being present help me to allow that relationship to actually be in a positive place in my life. And you have the right to zip it and walk away when things get bad. Who else came up with some victories, little victories? Yes, Amy.

AMY

All right. Well, a friend of mine invited me to join her writing class. I just kept saying, "No, I'm terrified." I finally signed up for next month with her. And yeah, it's good. I'm nervous, though, because I've been like, "I'm not ready." That was a victory.

MARGIE

Writing is a great way to use your creativity. We're creators; we're not just actors, right? We can all stretch our creativity outside of our comfort zone.

MEL

So, last night, my brother said that he didn't think that anything was going to change in our political situation and racial issues in this country, that by next month it'll be another news cycle and it's all hopeless and what's the point. I challenged him and said: "Well, if you don't think anything's going to change and you do nothing, then you can guarantee that nothing's going to change. But you have two sons. How can you possibly just stay on the sidelines?" And after the call, I was sure my brother was going to stop talking to me. I couldn't sleep. I woke up early and looked at my phone, and there was a message from him, saying: "I apologize for my negativity. I don't know if things are going to change, but maybe they might." What a victory for us!

MARGIE

Most people stay in that fear zone to protect themselves. If you give me hope, then that's scary because what if it doesn't happen? So why do I want to enjoy myself now? Right? I will anticipate something good, and my expectations will rise. But the truth is hope gives us light and beautiful possibilities. That victory of hope is a really great place to be. Hope sets us free.

NIKKO

I have had so many wins in this class, and it has stemmed from letting go. Letting go of what the director/casting director/ producer is looking for, letting go of my preconceived notions of getting the "slice" right, and letting go of the judgment of myself. Most notably, the Playful Child and the Nurturing Parent have guided me to take more risks, to stretch my limits, and to remind me that everything is going to be okay. And as Margie has taught me, "Fuck it! Just do it!"

Risks can lead to great victories or defeats. Even if you are defeated, the lesson will be valuable for the next stage of life.

—Lailah Gifty Akita, inspirational writer and founder, Smart Youth Volunteers Foundation

Charles F. Porter's Story— The Nonessentials Shed Like a Snake's Skin

In 2010, at the ripe age of thirty, I was diagnosed with stage IV Hodgkin's lymphoma. On what felt like a fast track to fame and fortune, my life was flipped upside down. I graduated from Duke University in 2002. There I played Division I football at its highest level. Having faced off with and against national champions, contenders, Heisman trophy winners, first-round picks, and future Hall of Famers, I knew what it took to compete, and more important, I learned what it took to win. I left football to become an actor in Hollywood, where I met Margie. I had the false belief that all I had to do was show up. I found out what was missing was the person saying the lines. What was missing was me. I was not taking the risk that solidifies us as not only great artists, but as great human beings. I was scared to become the lead in my own life. Margie showed me exactly who she was, day one of our relationship. She stepped out of her comfort zone for me and anyone in earshot, and that was so appealing and powerful. I was too busy trying to "make it" in the business to just enjoy creating.

Here I stand with you as a ten-year cancer destroyer. I had a stem cell transplant in 2011, and I am in my third relapse. I have had what feels like every chemo under the sun and was even on a trial immunotherapy for three years. With each year, treatments improve so I fight to stay healthy, active, and positive. Nothing like a stage IV cancer diagnosis to bring you completely present into life right now. The nonessentials shed like a snake's skin. My first book of poems, *Get to Know: Unlocking the Essence in You*, describes the journey of my cancer battle and how fighting for my life brought me the answers that I sought about myself and the contribution I would give to life. All we have is now. Make the most of it.

THE SILVER LINING, MARY WILSON OF THE SUPREMES

My best friend, Mary Wilson, died suddenly and unexpectedly in February 2021. Shortly before she passed away, she sent me an email that spoke to me of her happy life philosophy. I am grateful I had her positive light in my own life for five decades. Mary made it her priority to be present, as you can read in her words:

I have had a life full of fun, but also full of ups and downs. I grew up singing every morning, looking at the beautiful stars in the sky. To me, even the billowing clouds were magnificent. I told myself that I would always hold on to the thought that life is beautiful.

My love for life was challenged by poverty and distrust, so I protected my true feelings, as they did not fit into what people were showing and telling me. But even at a young age, I never stopped thinking that there was a silver lining behind every cloud of tears. Life can throw you a lot of curves. It's how you move through them.

Even when I lost my baby in a car accident, or when I found out I was in an abusive marriage, or when the Supremes came to an end, I knew that I had to reach inside me to the beauty that I knew was there. Life is a gift, and I can choose to go on a journey of love and shift the lens to positivity.

I have always dared to dream, even when it was an impossible dream. As Popeye used to say, "I am what I am." I believe that is what has gotten me through my life, loving myself first and being true to myself.

OH, GEORGIE!

I look back at the wonderful journey I have taken over the past year. I have gotten to know myself deeper because of my commitment to this book. I've gained clarity on the struggles I went through in my youth when I realized I was gay. Keeping it a secret damaged my self-worth, which snowballed into a life of needing to be loved and accepted. It was a domino effect.

Through therapy and the catharsis of writing, I have learned invaluable lessons. There is no such thing as failure if I am out of my comfort zone. Only staying in it can stop me from growing. If I stumble, I will fall forward into an unknown and magical place, which will bring joy into my life. I have learned never to underestimate the impact of a small victory.

My students have taught me that there are countless journeys we can take in the quest for knowledge. Each road can bring you to a fascinating destination if you are willing to explore the ride. I cherish the times that I Zoom with my family. We have actually grown closer, and I see more of my family back East than I ever have. As I write the final lines of this book, I sit in my backyard, absorbing its beauty. I get to be present with my dog, Georgie. Oh, how much I love him! Georgie, a Tibetan terrier, isn't what one would call a lap dog. This stay-at-home lifestyle that happened during the COVID-19 pandemic has changed him as well. I find myself sitting on the lounge chair with Georgie's adorable head in my lap as he sighs with contentment, and we both bask in the stillness.

I used to love the adrenaline rush. How much can I do in one day? I thought if I spent all twenty-four hours of the day being productive, I would find happiness. But after the day was done, the adrenaline would fade, and I was just left there. Right there. By myself. With myself. No place to go. The time in confinement was my teacher. Now, I know what it means to just be. I'm good with me. I don't need someone or something else to fill me up.

Being present is the answer to extending my life, to finding true happiness. I can catch up to time instead of running away from it. Don't miss a second of each precious day we are given. F*ck your comfort zone! Be the lead in your life!

If we stay curious, we will thrive. If we are empathetic, we will develop loving relationships. It starts with loving ourselves. My Nurturing Parent every morning says to me: "Good morning, Margie. I love you. You are kind. You are loving. You are magnificent!" Let's all reach our arms up to the sky and open ourselves up to the incredible abundance of this planet!

I may not have avoided certain wounds in my life, but I do appreciate these scars because they are a constant reminder of my victories.

—Gift Gugu Mona, writer, poet, songwriter,
philosopher, and philanthropist

POWER CHALLENGE

- What three things about the future preoccupy your mind? Write about what your life might look like without these preoccupations.
- Fear knocks us out of the present. What fears are getting in your way? Write them down, then cross them off. Let them go.

- Write down a stressful situation that recently occurred in your life. Then write how you could get out of it through your senses and experiencing your body.
- List five bad habits and five actions to change them. How does this bring you more happiness?
- Do the imaginary cigarette exercise. Remember to close your eyes and do it very slowly. Now write down what it felt like to be present.
- Look around you and notice everything in the moment. Now write down all that you saw when you were being present and how it affected you.
- Remember the Playful Child? Dive into three ways to use your Playful Child to be present.
- Write down three times when you have said, "I'm happy because. . . ." Then replace them with, "It's just the way I like to live my life."
- Write about three incidents in which you have experienced little victories. Enjoy every one of them!

ACKNOWLEDGMENTS

Many wonderful people contributed to making this book possible:

My editors, James Mihaley (first draft) and Marcia Wilkie (final drafts), who both brilliantly helped me edit my book with love.

My friend Jeff Black, who published my first book, *How to Get the Part... Without Falling Apart!*, and has been my lifeline for so many years and who believed in my talent—thank you.

My darling friend Barbara Babchick, who has worked with me on the outline and was a constant supply of creative ideas. Also, Hamish Sturgeon, who manages my company, Margie Haber Studio, and, with great loyalty, supports my efforts, gives fantastic insight, and goes beyond the call of duty. Thank you both for your enduring friendships.

My agent Peter Miller, who passed away in 2021, will always be remembered for his generous spirit and passion. To my publisher, Judith Regan, who fell in love with me on a phone call and then championed my book through our madness—my sincere thanks. Much appreciation to photographers Steven Busby and Tracey Landworth for their beautiful photos. And a big thank you to artist Tim Manley for his creativity. Thank you to Richard Ljoenes for his exceptional, inspired work as a graphic designer.

To my colleagues, friends, students, and associates, who provided endorsements, and to the Margie Haber Studio teachers who are committed to excellence—my deepest appreciation.

This book is a tribute to my fantastic students, especially those in my Monday and Wednesday master classes, who willingly shared their personal journeys during this difficult pandemic.

I also want to thank my family, whom I love very much: my fabulous sisters, Lois and Joan; my beautiful wife, Susan; my wonderful son, Michael; and, of course, Georgie, my Tibetan terrier, who sat by my side as I wrote this book and who has always loved me unconditionally.

*

ABOUT THE AUTHOR

Margie Haber is a widely known and influential acting coach who lives and teaches in Los Angeles. Since the inception of the Margie Haber Studio twenty-five years ago, she has taught and trained thousands of actors; coached hundreds of corporate, religious, public, and political leaders; and led workshops across the United States and around the world, including in Brazil, Indonesia, Australia, India, Africa, and several European countries.

Making her debut on Broadway—not the one with theater marquees but a residential street on Long Island where she grew up—Margie has always been involved in entertainment. She has captivated audiences since she was four, when her father would encourage her to do her Ed Sullivan impression for guests. Margie charged through her childhood, singing unapologetically whether onstage or wandering down a sidewalk.

At a time when many college girls headed to Haight-Ashbury and the hippie movement, Margie was on the road with her best friend, Mary Wilson of Motown's megahit group Diana Ross & the Supremes. She attended concerts, went to events, and spent afternoons poolside in Los Angeles with Michael Jackson, Tom Jones, Lola Falana, Nancy Wilson, Leslie Uggams, the Temptations, the Four Tops, and many other stars of that era.

After observing people from all walks of life, Margie realized her best talent was giving actors and others the space and freedom to be creative, vulnerable, and authentic so they could step out of their comfort zones. She believes that this is how to really live life and stop "acting." New students and clients often seek out Margie because they are fearful, uptight, and full of rules and regulations about the "right" way to audition or do a presentation or make a speech. They leave with newfound energy, creativity, and a more authentic sense of self, which has proven to be very effective, both professionally and personally.

Margie raised her son, Michael, as a single mother while running her own successful business. She has held her place at the top of the go-to list for acting agencies and personal managers who refer their own clients to her on a daily basis. Her who's-who list of current and past celebrity clients includes Brad Pitt, Halle Berry, Tiffany Haddish, Mariska Hargitay, Kyle Chandler, Rick Springfield, Josh Duhamel, and many more. For two years in a row, Margie was the *Backstage* Readers' Choice Award winner for "Best Acting Coach," as voted on by readers and industry panels.

Margie's first book, *How to Get the Part . . . Without Falling Apart!*, is used throughout the world in drama schools and colleges, and is considered a great acting resource for its style and content. Margie has been featured in the *Hollywood Reporter, Variety, USA Today,* and *Backstage,* as well as articles for *Casting Frontier* and other major industry publications.

People trust Margie. Whether she is in the intimate setting of her acting intensives or wielding a microphone in front of hundreds of corporate clients, Margie shows people how to live in the unknown and find their personal power, happiness, and courage to be the lead in their own lives.

Margie lives in Los Angeles with her wife, Susan, and her constant and most adoring companion, her Tibetan terrier, Georgie.

179-150 peer
Art
200 Art
222 pen
little
victory

81360202R00134